DATE DUE

AG 10 '09			

Healing

the

Wounds

DAVID M. NOER

Healing

OVERCOMING

THE TRAUMA OF LAYOFFS

AND REVITALIZING DOWNSIZED

the

ORGANIZATIONS

Wounds

Jossey-Bass Publishers
San Francisco

Substantial discounts on bulk quantities of Jossey-Bass books
are available to corporations, professional associations, and other
organizations. For details and discount information, contact the
special sales department at Jossey-Bass Inc., Publishers.
(415) 433-1740; Fax (415) 433-0499.

For international orders, please contact your local Paramount Publishing
International office.

Manufactured in the United States of America

The paper used in this book is acid-free and meets the
State of California requirements for recycled paper
(50 percent recycled waste, including 10 percent
postconsumer waste), which are the strictest guidelines
for recycled paper currently in use in the United States.

10% POST
CONSUMER
WASTE

Library of Congress Cataloging-in-Publication Data

Noer, David M., date.
    Healing the wounds : overcoming the trauma of layoffs and
revitalizing downsized organizations / David M. Noer. — 1st ed.
        p.   cm. — (The Jossey-Bass management series)
    Includes bibliographical references and index.
    ISBN 1-55542-560-7
    1. Organizational change—Psychological aspects. 2. Unemploy-
ment—Psychological aspects. 3. Employees—Dismissal of. I. Title.
II. Series.
HM131.N63   1993
302.3′5—dc20   93-13407
                                                                CIP

FIRST EDITION
HB Printing   10 9 8 7 6 5 4   *Code 9368*

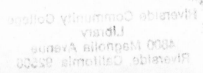

The Jossey-Bass

Management Series

Contents

Preface

Some years ago, I visited an old friend I had not seen in almost a year. It was a crisp, clear autumn afternoon, the kind of day that makes you walk a little faster and smile a little quicker. I was looking forward both to seeing him and to renewing my acquaintance with the organization in which he was vice president of marketing, a small but exciting high-technology spin-off from a large multinational corporation. The last time I had visited, this vibrant company had been just three years old. Its five hundred employees were turned on, bureaucracy was turned off, and you could feel the energy; the organization was brimming over with work spirit and creativity.

But things had changed. The open, cheerful, smiling faces had been replaced by tense, rigid masks. A good consultant gathers useful data just by walking organizational corridors, and I had picked up some distressing nonverbal messages on my way to my friend's office. The delightful, almost playful tone of the organization that I remembered had turned somber, almost sullen.

The first thing my friend did was to hand me his résumé; next he told me about the past nine months. The venture capitalists who had bankrolled the spin-off were unhappy with the financial results and had brought in a new president. He was a "turnaround" expert, which meant that his first step was to institute significant across-the-board layoffs. In the ensuing six months, several more waves of reductions took place. Now there were too few people and too much work, and the organization was in a steep decline. I was amazed at the drastic change in organizational culture. After a brief tour, I had had enough. The people who had survived the reductions were clearly fearful, angry, and depressed. Yet this was the same work force that was expected to turn the organization around and meet global competition!

"I hope you sold your charter stock," I told my friend as I walked out the door. The sun was setting behind some clouds and the chill I felt was due as much to my organizational encounter as to the weather.

As I walked to my car, I reflected on the rapidity with which an organization that had once brimmed over with creative, dynamic spirit and pleasure and even joy in work had been reduced to a place filled with sullen and angry survivors. I didn't know it at the time, but I had had my first face-to-face encounter with what I was later to name *layoff survivor sickness*.

Since that time more than ten years ago, organizations of all types — public, private, military, for-profit, not-for-profit — have embarked on a frenzy of layoffs. Organizations that once saw people as assets to be nurtured and developed began to view those same people as costs to be cut. Employees who took job security for granted and expected to be taken care of in return for their work and loyalty have had to face a new reality in which organizations can no longer provide long-term employment or career paths or foster employees' sense of self-worth. Downsizings resulted in layoffs. Restructurings resulted in layoffs. Productivity improvement programs resulted in layoffs. Mergers resulted in layoffs. Higher energy costs resulted in layoffs. Foreign competition resulted in layoffs, and on and on!

Every day the media pour out reports of old, stable organizations putting long-term employees out on the street.

Many organizations have done a good job in outplacement, spending time and money to help those who have left. Very little is done for those who stay behind, the survivors who have the task of revitalizing the organization. *Healing the Wounds* deals with this forgotten but vital group. My purpose is to explain the nature of layoff survivor sickness and to help both individuals and organizations formulate strategies to fight off this disease.

Layoff survivor sickness is widespread and toxic to both the human spirit and organizational survival. Organizations institute layoffs to cut costs and promote competitiveness but afterward often find themselves worse off than before. All they have gained is a depressed, anxious, and angry work force. At the very time they need spirit and creativity, they enter into global competition with a risk-averse team. At the individual level, a changing social paradigm and the unfolding of a new psychological employment contract has left many layoff survivors confused, fearful, and unable to shake an unhealthy and unreciprocated organizational dependency.

AUDIENCE

Although anyone interested in the profound changes taking place in the relationship of person to organization will find *Healing the Wounds* useful, I have directed my comments toward three often overlapping audiences: organizational managers and leaders, layoff survivors, and layoff victims.

Organizational Managers and Leaders

If you are a manager or leader in an organization that has been, or is about to be, downsized, you have a tremendously important role and a difficult twofold task. First, you must come to grips with your own survivor status. You must deal with your own feelings while you work toward a relationship with your organization in which you are more empowered and less dependent. You cannot be of much help to other layoff survivors until you have helped yourself. Second, you must take on the most vital and complex managerial role since the industrial revolution. You must lead the other people in your organization through the current painful but irrevocable shift in the terms of the psychological contract that exists between employee and organization.

This book can help you reach a personal understanding and acceptance of your own survivor feelings while also providing insight into the ways employees can develop a more autonomous and less dependent organizational relationship. Chapters Seven, Eight, and Nine provide examples of managerial actions that support the new psychological employment contract, which no longer guarantees job security.

Chapters Ten and Eleven provide an important frame of reference for those striving to understand the basic shifts taking place in the new reality. Many organizational leaders feel a great deal of pain and guilt over what they perceive they have done to employees in the service of organizational downsizing. These chapters help alleviate this guilt by pointing out that the organizational changes are systemic. Managers who previewed these chapters have reported feeling relieved that their current problems lie in a pervasive change in the overall system and not with them as individuals.

If you are a manager, you are caught up in a basic change in the relationship of individuals to organizations, and you are asked to play a vital leadership role during this painful transition. You must lead the change from within the change. This book will help you deal with your own survivor issues and frame the environmental changes underlying downsizing; it will help alleviate guilt you may feel for what you have "done to" employees; and it will offer practical ideas for exercising leadership in the midst of fundamental change.

Layoff Survivors

If you are among the increasing legions of people who remain in organizations that have been downsized, merged, or "delayered," *Healing the Wounds* will help you understand that you are not alone. The anxiety, fear, and sometimes depression that you experience are normal survivor feelings. However, many who survive cutbacks work in organizational cultures that do not permit individuals to admit to natural survivor reactions. Even in organizations where emotions are considered valid data, it is difficult for most people to be truly open about their survivor feelings. After cutbacks, there is great if often subtle pressure to dig in, tighten your belt, grit your teeth, and work harder to move the organization forward. In macho post-layoff cultures, people feel it would be selfish or not teamlike to admit their true anguish and say how debilitating that anguish is.

If you are a layoff survivor, the most immediate benefit of this book may well be a clearer understanding of your normal and yet often unshared survivor feelings. The first three chapters show why those who survive layoffs universally feel such a deep sense of violation. In Chapters Four and Five, readers will discover both personal and organizational echoes in the actual voices of layoff survivors. While Chapters Four and Five legitimize survivors' repressed feelings and begin a necessary catharsis, Chapter Nine points the way for survivors and victims alike toward breaking an unhealthy organizational dependency and learning to create an empowered employment relationship, with reduced susceptibility to layoff survivor sickness.

If you are among those who remain after cutbacks, *Healing the Wounds* will help you toward a deeper understanding and acceptance of your survivor symptoms and give you strategies for an employment relationship in which you are more autonomous and less likely to feel like a victim.

Layoff Victims

Most layoff victims, those who have left involuntarily, eventually find themselves employed in another organization. A surprising number, particularly managers and professionals, rebound into organizations with worse epidemics of layoff survivor sickness than those the layoff victims came from. In this way, many employees simply transport their survivor symptoms from one place to another.

I have a friend, now in his third organization, who reports feeling less enthusiastic with each successive move. When it comes to life planning, his scarce and marketable skills, good network, and interviewing savvy ironically have made it easy for him to rebound. He has not taken the time to deal with his survivor feelings, to take stock of what he really wants to do, or to come to grips with the reality of the new employment contract, which calls for a more autonomous, less dependent employment relationship.

If you are a layoff victim, you must make your transition a learning experience. An understanding of the nature of the new employment contract (Chapter Ten), of the personal perils of organizational dependency (Chapter Nine), of the survivor symptoms that probably exist in many of the organizations to which you are applying (Chapter Four), and of the ways you can manage your transition (Chapter Eleven) will be of great help in your personal transition.

OVERVIEW OF THE CONTENTS

Both individuals and organizations must understand that layoff survivor sickness debilitates them. Organizations should develop systems to accommodate the new linkages that are called for between individuals and organizations. Individuals should develop more entrepreneurial and less dependent connections to organizations. What is at stake is nothing less than the survival of our organizations and of our self-esteem and autonomy as employees. That survival is also the subject of this book.

Although research in the field is increasing, layoff survivor sickness is not well understood or studied. Because denial is a primary symptom of the sickness, its effects are nearly always underestimated. Moreover, the higher a person is in an organizational system, the more he or she denies the symptoms. For these reasons, I devote the first half of the book to an explanation of the pathology of layoff survivor sickness. In the remainder of the book, I show what to do about the sickness, using a four-level intervention model.

I have divided the book into four parts. In Part One, I outline the profound changes in the relationship of person to job that leads to the mistrust and sense of violation felt by the survivors of organizational layoffs. Chapter One examines the dynamics of layoff survivor sickness through a case study and a metaphor. Chapter Two outlines the fundamental paradigm shift that has occurred in the relationship of person to organization.

The universality of the survivor experience and the similarities between the feelings of layoff survivors and the feelings of survivors of other traumatic situations is the subject of Part Two. Chapter Three explores the universal traits of survivorship, to demonstrate that there are emotional links between layoff survivors and others who have survived trauma and tragedy. Archetypal survivor themes emerge that are also apparent in the statements of actual layoff survivors.

Most research on layoff survivors is conducted in a laboratory or is a summary of questionnaire results. Chapter Four presents raw data from actual layoff survivors, to bring home to the reader the depth and complexity of layoff survivor symptoms. It will be a rare person who is not reminded of his or her own organizational situation. The host organization for the research sample in Chapter Four was revisited five years later, and the results of a second sample are presented in Chapter Five. It is apparent that, unlike wine, layoff survivors do not automatically improve with age!

Part Three is centered around a new four-level intervention model that serves as a road map to reestablishing healthy and productive relationships between employees and organizations in the midst of continual downsizing and post-layoff trauma. Chapter Six sums up the research and introduces the four-level intervention model, a method of dealing with research results. Chapter Seven explores Level 1, or process, interventions. These are basic first aid interventions at the point when layoffs take place. Level 1 interventions will not cure layoff survivor sickness but will provide damage control until more permanent solutions are found.

Layoff survivors carry heavy emotional baggage and unless given the opportunity to drop it, are unable to progress beyond their debilitating funk. Level 2 interventions allow survivors to grieve. Chapter Eight outlines processes for breaking blockages and stimulating catharsis.

Chapter Nine applies the concept of codependency to organizations. Level 3 interventions deal with the painful but liberating process of breaking away from organizational codependency. Employees are codependent with an organization to the extent that they index their self-worth by their success in that organization and attempt to control and manipulate the organizational system. Organizationally codependent people are always susceptible to layoff survivor sickness. Those who break the bonds of organizational codependency are immune.

Level 4 interventions alter organizational systems to accommodate the reality of the new employment contract. Chapter Ten reviews the series of shifts that have made a new employment contract necessary. It explores processes for making organizational systems relevant to the new contract, which demands changes both in our organizational systems and in us as individuals. The changes are profound and evolutionary. On the personal level, they often require us to behave in accordance with a reality that opposes the values conditioned into us over the past fifty years.

In discussing Levels 1 and 2 (Chapters Seven and Eight), I have been as prescriptive as possible, and I have included case studies and specific advice to both the employee and the manager. My advice is more general for Levels 3 and 4 (Chapters Nine and Ten). Implementing the new employment contract demands complex individual and organizational changes. Therefore, I help readers explore the changes in their own organizations and personal careers.

Part Four deals with the critical leadership challenges within this new environment of change, ambiguity, and violated employee expectations of long-term job security. Today's leadership requires new skills and a great deal of courage. Chapter Eleven examines leadership competencies relevant in the new reality.

The death of the old patterns of organizational thought and behavior, painful though it may be, opens up the possibility that we as individuals will acquire greater personal empowerment and autonomy and that more organizations will survive these competitive times. Chapter Twelve discusses the ultimate existential choices that individuals and organizations now confront.

Appendix A provides details on the demographics and methodology of the survivor study described in Chapter Four. (The demographics and differences in methodology of the follow-up study are described in the introductory paragraphs of Chapter Five.) Appendix B describes the methodology and outcomes of a study of human resource professionals who had been heavily involved in layoff administration.

Since I encountered the grim and unfortunate organization where my friend worked, layoff survivor sickness has been a part of my consulting practice, my research, and my writing. *Healing the Wounds* is the culmination of multiple ways of perceiving and responding to the syndrome. It combines research, case studies, and methodologies from my own consulting practice, and specific advice based on my experience. The case studies have been disguised, to "protect the innocent" and ensure client anonymity. As a practitioner's book, it can be used at several levels: to help line managers intervene in their organizational systems, to help consultants and consulting managers develop intervention techniques, and to help individual survivors understand what is happening to them and see that they are not alone. As a report on research, it can be used by researchers and theory builders seeking a context for further work.

In the final analysis, *Healing the Wounds* views layoff survivor sickness as the symptom of a condition even more toxic to the human spirit: unhealthy dependence. For those who respond courageously to the wake-up call to combat this symptom, there is the exciting promise of reclamation of lost autonomy and the ability to index self-worth by good work, rather than by fitting into an organization.

Greensboro, North Carolina   David M. Noer
June 1993

Acknowledgments

I must thank all my clients who took a risk and joined with me to form learning communities, despite my initially often clumsy and untested methods. Those clients have taught me much. I also want to thank the people at Gantz-Wiley Research for their good work.

There are two Walters in my life who are very special: Walter Ulmer, a new-paradigm boss and role model, who encouraged me to write this book amidst the normal overload of managing a dynamic and vibrant organization; and my friend and colleague Walter Tornow, who does not know that I know how much of a mentor he has been to me over the years. A special thanks to Deborah Kyre, whose tireless efforts and gentle help have translated my manic scribbles and "interesting" typing into these pages. Most of all, I want to thank my wife, Diana, for giving me the time and the space, including many late nights and weekends, to get this book out of my head, out of my heart, and onto these pages.

Since I now work for that wonderful organization the Center for Creative Leadership, I must also point out that I heard most of the client stories earlier in my career and that the opinions in this book are mine and not necessarily shared by all my colleagues or representative of center policy.

D.M.N.

The Author

David M. Noer is currently vice president for training and education at the Center for Creative Leadership, with worldwide responsibility for the center's training and educational activities. His professional interests, apart from assistance to layoff survivors, are focused on breaking individuals' codependent relationships with organizations to create employee autonomy, peak effectiveness among executives, new-paradigm leadership, and healthier, more competitive organizations.

Before joining the Center for Creative Leadership, Noer was president of his own consulting firm, specializing in work force revitalization, executive development, and strategic planning. Much of his work helped executive teams and organizational systems deal with the effects of layoffs on employees who remained behind.

Noer has also held positions as dean of the Control Data Academy of Management and as vice president of human resource development for the same organization, with responsibilities for succession planning, executive development, human resource research, and organizational development.

He has served as president and chief executive officer of Business Advisors, a Control Data subsidiary specializing in technology-based management consulting, with offices in the United States, England, and Australia. In addition to managing the firm, Noer provided diagnostic and developmental organizational consulting to executives in various client systems, particularly to executives dealing with the human implications of restructuring, downsizing, and layoffs.

Noer has also served as senior vice president of personnel and administration for Commercial Credit Company, a holding company with operating units in the fields of insurance, finance, consumer lending, banking, leasing, and real estate. In addition, he has held line and staff positions in the United States, Europe, and Asia.

Noer is the author of many articles on consulting skills, individual and executive development, and international human resource management. He has written three other books: *Multinational People Management* (1975), *How to Beat the Employment Game* (1975), and *Jobkeeping* (1976).

He received his B.A. degree (1962) in psychology and history from Gustavus Adolphus College; his M.S. degree (1979) in organizational development from Pepperdine University; and his D.B.A. degree (1988) in business administration, with a concentration in organizational behavior and a supporting field of executive mental health, from George Washington University.

He has served as adjunct faculty member at St. Thomas University and is a member of several professional associations. He also served on the board of trustees for the Organizational Development Network and was editor of the journal *OD Practitioner*.

Healing

the

Wounds

Part One

The

Shattered

Covenant

1

Forgotten Survivors: What Happens to Those Who Are Left Behind

"No one is happy anymore. I think a lot of
people are under stress, and it tends to
balloon out and everybody is absorbed by it.
You don't have anybody coming in in the
morning, going, 'God, it's a great day!'"

It begins with a deep sense of
violation. It often ends with angry, sad, and depressed employees, consumed with their attempt to hold on to jobs that
have become devoid of joy, spontaneity, and personal relevancy, and with the organization attempting to thrive in a
competitive global environment with a risk-averse, depressed
work force. This is no way to lead a life, and no way to run
an organization.

The root cause of layoff survivor sickness is a profound
shift in the psychological employment contract that binds individual and organization. The symptoms of layoff survivor
sickness are found in pockets in most organizations and are

breaking out in epidemic proportions in many. The battle to ward off and eventually develop an immunity to these survivor symptoms must be waged simultaneously by individuals and organizations. This battle is among the most important struggles that we and our organizations will ever face. Individuals must break the chains of their unhealthy, outdated organizational codependency and recapture their self-esteem; organizations must achieve their potential and thrive in the new world economy. For the organization, holding on to the familiar old is not the answer. For the individual, holding on to the job is not always the most healthy option, as the following examples illustrate.

JUANITA AND CHARLES: VICTIM AND SURVIVOR

When the layoffs hit, Juanita and Charles were both department directors, the lower end of the upper-management spectrum in the high-technology firm where they worked. Juanita was in her late forties, Charles in his early fifties. Although they had traversed very different paths to their management jobs, they were equally devastated when their organization started "taking out" managers to reduce costs. They experienced similar feelings of personal violation when the implicit psychological contract between each of them and their organization went up in smoke. Although this contract was only implied, Juanita and Charles had assumed that the organization shared their belief in the importance of this contract. It wasn't long before they were both experiencing survivor symptoms of fear, anxiety, and mistrust.

Juanita had achieved her management role. She had returned to school in midcareer, earned an MBA, and—through talent, determination, and the efforts of a good mentor—moved quickly through Anglo-male management ranks that were lonely and uncharted for a woman. Juanita eventually lost her job. The official explanation was that her department was "eliminated" and no other "suitable" positions were available. In reality, she was done in by the existing old boy network, which at least in the early stages of the layoffs, looked after its own. (In a form of layoff poetic justice, the network fell apart as the "rightsizing" continued.) Juanita was a "layoff victim."

Charles evolved into his management role. He was a classic organization man, joining the company right out of college and following the traditional career path of working his way up the system by punching the right tickets, knowing the right people, wearing the right clothes, and generally walking the walk and talking the talk. Such a career path was a hallmark of the large hierarchical organizations that dominated the post–World-War-II era in the United States. The psychological contract that Charles and Juanita trusted was a legacy of this company-endorsed career path. Charles believed he had made a covenant that, unless he violated the norms and standards of his company, he could count on his job until he retired or decided to leave. Although Charles has lost his influence, watched his support network disintegrate, and lives in a constant state of anxiety, guilt, and fear, he has managed to hang on. He is still with the organization, but he is now a layoff survivor, and he suffers from layoff survivor sickness. However, the company has no strategy to deal with his sickness.

When Juanita was laid off, the company helped her take stock of her life and career. It spent some time and a fair amount of money on her psychological counseling and outplacement services. Juanita took over two years to grope her way through a time of exploration, regeneration, and ambiguity that William Bridges (1980) has called the "neutral zone." She has now emerged as a principal in a small but vibrant and thriving consulting firm. She is excited about life, stimulated by her work, and has merged her career and personal life into a balance she found impossible in her previous job. She has become a much more integrated and congruent person since she became a layoff victim.

Charles is still living a marginally productive and anxiety-ridden life. His guilt, fear, and anger have spilled outside the job. He is emotionally isolated and has a growing chemical dependency. His behavior is alienating his family and friends. More than two years after the initial layoffs, he took part in a survivor support group, which was neither funded or sanctioned by his organization. Because the company helped those who left but paid no attention to the survivors, it had a risk-averse, angry, guilty, and nonproductive employee. In fact, this company had a whole building full of angry, nonproductive employees!

THE BASIC BIND: LEAN AND MEAN LEADS TO SAD AND ANGRY

Layoffs are intended to reduce costs and promote an efficient, lean and mean organization. However, what tends to result is a sad and angry organization, populated by depressed survivors. The basic bind is that the process of reducing staff to achieve increased efficiency and productivity often creates conditions that lead to the opposite result — an organization that is risk averse and less productive. The key variable is the survivors' sense of personal violation. The greater their perception of violation, the greater their susceptibility to survivor sickness. The perception of violation appears directly related to the degree of trust employees have had that the organization will take care of them. Since nearly all organizations of the past had strategies of taking care of their employees, this basic bind is alive and well (Figure 1.1).

One symptom of layoff survivor sickness is a hierarchical denial pattern: the higher a person resides in an organization, the more he or she will be invested in denying the symptoms of the sickness. This is one of the reasons that managers are often reluctant to implement intervention strategies, despite the increasing evidence of an epidemic of survivor symptoms,

Figure 1.1. The Basic Bind.

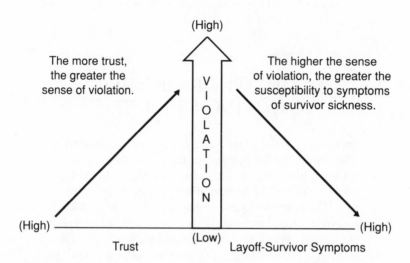

despite entire organizations filled with people like Charles. Understanding and dealing with survivor symptoms requires personal vulnerability and an emotional and spiritual knowledge of the symptoms. Most top managers are excellent at playing the role they and their employees have colluded to give them. Their egos require that they present an image of cool control and that they appear skilled and comfortable with rational and analytical knowing rather than emotional knowing. The management job in a downsized organization is extremely complex and demanding.

Managers and organizational leaders play a vital role in bringing about the emotional release necessary to begin the survivors' post-layoff healing process. Their denial must be dealt with before there can be any release. In my experience, confronting denial head-on only serves to reinforce it. Methods that help people reach out to and legitimize their emotions and spiritual feelings are more useful in helping these people to understand the dynamics of their layoff-survivor sickness. For example, I find that the following meta-

phor of the surviving children is a compelling way to demonstrate the emotional context of survivor sickness to managers
and help them move past denial.

METAPHOR OF THE
SURVIVING CHILDREN

Imagine a family: a father, a mother, and four children.
The family has been together for a long time, living in
a loving, nurturing, trusting environment. The parents
take care of the children, who reciprocate by being good.

Every morning the family sits down to breakfast
together, a ritual that functions as a bonding experience,
somewhat akin to an organizational staff meeting. One
morning, the children sense that something is wrong.
The parents exchange furtive glances, appear nervous,
and after a painful silence, the mother speaks. "Father
and I have reviewed the family budget," she says, looking down at her plate, avoiding eye contact, "and we just
don't have enough money to make ends meet!" She
forces herself to look around the table and continues,
"As much as we would like to, we just can't afford to
feed and clothe all four of you. After another silence she
points a finger. "You two must go!"

"It's nothing personal," explains the father as he
passes out a sheet of paper to each of the children. "As
you can see by the numbers in front of you, it's simply
an economic decision—we really have no choice." He
continues, forcing a smile, "We have arranged for your
aunt and uncle to help you get settled, to aid in your
transition."

The next morning, the two remaining children are
greeted by a table on which only four places have been
set. Two chairs have been removed. All physical evidence of the other two children has vanished. The emotional evidence is suppressed and ignored. No one talks
about the two who have disappeared. The parents em-

phasize to the two remaining children, the survivors, that they should be grateful, "since, after all, you've been allowed to remain in the family." To show their gratitude, the remaining children will be expected to work harder on the family chores. The father explains that "the workload remains the same even though there are two less of you." The mother reassures them that "this will make us a closer family!"

"Eat your breakfast, children," entreats the father. "After all, food costs money!"

After telling this story, I first ask surviving managers to reflect individually on the following five questions. Then I ask the managers to form small groups to discuss and amplify their answers.

1. *What were the children who left feeling?* Most managers say, "anger," "hurt," "fear," "guilt," and "sadness."

2. *What were the children who remained feeling?* Most managers soon conclude that the children who remain have the same feelings as those who left. The managers also often report that the remaining children experience these feelings with more intensity than those who left.

3. *What were the parents feeling?* Although the managers sometimes struggle with this question, most of them discover that the parents feel the same emotions as the surviving children.

4. *How different are these feelings from those of survivors in your organization?* After honest reflection, many managers admit that there are striking and alarming similarities.

5. *How productive is a work force with these survivor feelings?* Most managers conclude that such feelings are indeed a barrier to productivity. Some groups move into discussions about effects of survivor feelings on the quality of work life and share personal reflections.

What most managers take away from the metaphor of the children is a powerful and often personally felt understanding of the radical change the managers are experiencing in their own organizations. The vast majority of managers were hired into organizations that encouraged employees to feel as part of a family while managers performed the benevolent parent role. The reward for such performance was that all organizational employees, from executives to production people, would be taken care of. The harsh reality of the new psychological contract is that many "family" members are no longer cared for and are treated as dispensable commodities. It is not my intent to label this situation as good or bad. It is a sad situation for many, and it is a real situation for everyone. The fact that the old "family" contract is ending and the new competitive realities are creating a fundamental shift in the relationship of individual and organization. Managers and nonmanagers alike are part of this fundamental change in the system. It is ways of responding to this change, ways of making it good rather than bad, that I am concerned with here.

ISSUES TO BE EXPLORED

Metaphors or analogies tease out underlying issues and move them past our defense mechanisms. The metaphor of the surviving children allows survivors to bypass their denial. They begin to understand the dynamics of layoff survivor sickness by looking at the symptoms through the experience of others. This metaphor, along with the stories of Juanita and Charles, illustrates the following layoff survivor issues, which will be explored in this book.

Common Symptoms
Those who remain in hierarchical organizations after layoffs share feelings of anger, fear, anxiety, and distrust. These feelings are particularly strong when the organizations have been

nurturing and have captured the spirit of their employees. Employees have these feelings regardless of employment level. In the metaphor, the children and the parents shared the same feelings. In real organizations those in the executive suite and on the assembly line share similar survivor feelings.

Norm of Denial

Employees follow a norm of denying and blocking layoff survivor symptoms. This psychic numbing is also commonly found in survivors of other forms of trauma. The chain of denial among layoff survivors is difficult to break systematically because it is hierarchical: the higher the employee's rank, the stronger the denial. Denial also seems to be stronger in those who must actively plan and implement layoffs. Human resource people, for example, often seem to exhibit a "Judas complex." They engage in extensive rationalization and explanation to justify work force reductions. If there were a character equivalent to a human resource person in the surviving children metaphor, that character would be a caring aunt, uncle, or cousin who planned the separation, helped decide who would go, and either scripted or delivered the layoff notifications. That character would present rational arguments as to the economic need for the downsizing.

Shared Symptoms Among Survivors and Victims

The feelings of those who stay and those who leave are mirror images of each other. There is, in fact, some evidence that the terms could reasonably be reversed: those who leave become survivors, and those who stay become victims.

Helping Resources Restricted to Those Who Leave

As the example of Juanita and Charles illustrated, the laid-off employee, Juanita, was helped by life and career counseling, outplacement assistance, and a variety of transitional support services; all of which were paid for by the organization. But the survivor, Charles, was expected to report to work the next morning as though nothing happened, be grateful, and work harder. A strong norm of denial within the organization made him suppress his anger. The suppression resulted in survivor guilt, depression, and in Charles's case, alcohol abuse. The organization devoted no resources to help Charles deal with his layoff-survivor sickness.

Long-Term Symptoms

The literature about survivors clearly shows that survivor feelings are long term. Although much more research is needed, current evidence indicates that layoff survivors are no different than survivors of other forms of tragedy in that their symptoms do not go away unaided.

Needed Intervention Strategies

The family in the metaphor was a system in need of an intervention. Given the persistence of survivor symptoms, the norm of denial, and the general atmosphere of risk avoidance, the people in an organizational family will also tend to lock into a pattern of codependency with their survivorship. This codependency is also change resistant and persists over time. Multilevel intervention strategies at both the individual and systems levels are needed to break this unhealthy and counterproductive pattern.

DEFINITIONS

Layoff survivor sickness and the organizational realities that accompany this sickness are a relatively new topic in management writings. Some of the terminology is also new. These are the definitions of the terms I use to help people understand layoff-survivor sickness and the new realities.

Layoff. The term *layoff* is used generically to refer to all involuntary employee reductions for causes other than performance. Layoff in this sense does not imply that the employee may be recalled when business improves. Other common terms that convey the same meaning are *reduction-in-force* and *termination.* I do not use *firing* because it implies poor performance.

Layoff Survivor Sickness. Layoff survivor sickness is a generic term that describes a set of attitudes, feelings, and perceptions that occur in employees who remain in organizational systems following involuntary employee reductions. Words commonly used to describe the symptoms of layoff survivor sickness are *anger, depression, fear, distrust,* and *guilt.* People with survivor sickness have often been described as having a reduced desire to take risks, a lowered commitment to the job, and a lack of spontaneity.

Victim. The term *layoff victim* is used in this book and is beginning to be used in both academic and popular literature to refer to the person who involuntarily leaves the organization, who is laid off. I hope to show how organization can be "lean and mean" without creating people who feel victimized.

Survivor. Layoff survivors are those people who remain in organizational systems after involuntary employee reductions. The boundary between victims and survivors is blurred, however, because survivors often behave as survivor-victims.

Old Employment Contract. This is the psychological contract that implies that employees who perform and fit into the culture can count on a job until they retire or choose to leave.

New Employment Contract. This psychological contract fits the new reality. It says that even the best performer or the most culturally adaptive person cannot count on long-term employment. It replaces loyalty to an organization with loyalty to one's work.

Organizational Codependency. The concept of codependency originated in the treatment of alcoholism. It has since been expanded to other addictive relationships. It is used here to describe the employee's relationship with an organization under the old employment contract.

Old Paradigm. This is the broad context, or setting, within which the old employment contract was played out.

It describes the boundaries or limits we once used to understand organizations, employees, and their relationship.

New Paradigm. This is the broad context within which the new employment contract is manifested. *New paradigm* describes the boundaries of a new way of understanding employees, organizations, and their relationship.

Good Work. This term describes task-specific behavior from which individuals derive worth, self-esteem, and value. *Good work* is part of the new employment contract.

Survivor Guilt. The term *survivor guilt* describes a fundamental condition that leads to, and is often expressed in terms of, other survivor symptoms, such as depression, fear, or anger. In the context of layoff survivor sickness, *guilt* may be generally defined as "a feeling of responsibility or remorse for some offense; an emotional reaction that one has violated social mores" (Gottesfeld, 1979, p. 525).

LEARNINGS AND IMPLICATIONS

The real stories of Juanita and Charles and the metaphor of the surviving children illustrate the dynamics of layoff survivor sickness. These stories introduced themes I will explore in future chapters: the denial chain, shared symptoms among survivors and victims, the propensity of organizations to help those who leave and take for granted those who remain, the persistence of survivor symptoms, and the necessity for intervention strategies.

Before individuals or organizations can formulate healing strategies, they need a deep literal and symbolic understanding of the pathology of layoff survivor sickness. To help managers avoid the trap of instant diagnosis, or the ready, fire, aim strategy to which many Western organizations often succumb, the next five chapters will explore the depth and breadth of this sickness. Chapter Two begins this process with a review of the fundamental change in the relationship of people to organizations, the change that is causing such agony today.

2

Changing Organizations
and the End
of Job Security

"The only way you provide security for
yourself is by making sure that your work
experience is as up-to-date as possible so that
if tomorrow happens, you are able to go out
and get another job because you have skills
people want. That's the only way you have
security. You aren't going to get it from the
company. It will never be that way again."

I have a colleague whose sec-
ond least favorite word is *empowerment*. At the top of his list
is *paradigm*. While both words have recently been overused
and misused, I use them a great deal in this book because
they still convey powerful and unique meanings. The profound and basic change in the typical relationship between
employee and organization, and between organization and
society, is nothing less than the fundamental change in worldview envisioned by Thomas Kuhn (1970) when he rescued
the word *paradigm* from obscurity. We *are* in the midst of a
fundamental paradigm shift. This chapter will examine that

shift in detail, because both individuals attempting to shake the symptoms of layoff-survivor sickness and regain meaning and relevance in their work and organizations struggling to compete in the new global economy need to understand the significance of this basic shift. Although it is difficult to see change when we are in the middle of it, there are four organizational yardsticks we can use to measure it. These yardsticks have an old worldview at one end and a new worldview at the other (see Figure 1.2.) The changes they measure occur in the assumptions organizations make about the purpose of employees, the language patterns organizations use to talk about employees, the long-term versus short-term time orientation of organizations, and the optimum operational size of organizations.

FROM ASSETS TO COSTS: THE NEW VIEW OF EMPLOYEES

Perhaps the clearest evidence of the paradigm shift is that organizations that used to perceive people as long-term assets to be nurtured and developed now see people as short-term costs to be reduced. This basic change has a radical impact on the staffing and development cycle (hiring, training, career planning, and succession planning). Even more important, it represents a fundamental shift in the psychological covenant between the organization and the individual. Under the values of the old contract, employees in most large business, military, government, and religious hierarchies were perceived as assets to be nurtured and grown (often through organizational training and developmental programs) over the long term. Even Frederick Taylor's "scientific management," mechanistic though it was, never envisioned a throwaway employee. Employees, like machines, were intended to be properly fit into the system, tuned, lubricated, and maintained over the long haul. Today, many organizations view people

Figure 2.1. Paradigm Shifts.

Old and New Assumptions About People

From	To
People as assets to be developed:	People as costs to be reduced:
Grow and cultivate	Hire and cut

Old and New Language Patterns

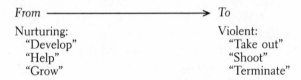

From	To
Nurturing:	Violent:
"Develop"	"Take out"
"Help"	"Shoot"
"Grow"	"Terminate"

Old and New Time Orientation

From	To
Long term:	Short term:
A career	A job
Make an employee	Buy an employee

Old and New Size Orientation

From	To
Synergistic:	Reductionist:
Build up	Make smaller
Develop	Cut

as "things" that are but one variable in the production equation, "things" that can be discarded when the profit and loss numbers do not come out as desired. However, unlike machines, people who are discarded have a significant effect on those who remain within the system.

"They Believed 'til the Door Hit Them in the Ass on the Way Out!"

A common employee response to the shift in organizational viewpoint is captured in the bitter words of Tony, a human resource manager who helped plan layoffs during the mid-eighties until he was laid off himself. He is now working as a manufacturer's representative. During his interview, he said:

> Now that I'm out, I can see how things really changed — and not for the better! It sounded like God and motherhood, but we really meant it. In the early days, back in the seventies, we said people were the most important things. Without good people, there wouldn't be an organization. The thing is we really believed that BS and acted on it. We paid well, sent a lot of people to school — we had a super tuition refund process, lots of internal training and management development. We were in the human resource development business. It was part of everything we did. In the last few years, all we did was cut, cut, cut. They didn't give a damn about development. It was cut your head count, look for ways to get people out — the old meat grinder. The thing is, some of the lifers, the old-timers, still believed in all that crap — believed it 'til the door hit them in the ass on the way out! Talk about walking your talk: when we were cutting the hell out of the place — taking out whole layers, functions — we still said that people were most important. What a crock!

Organizational Planning for "Inhuman" Resources

Another clue to the paradigm shift in the way organizations view employees has surfaced in an exercise I use with clients. A few years ago, as part of a post–merger/layoff planning session, I asked managers to write a paper contrasting their organizational considerations and decision-making processes for purchasing or leasing a facility with those for hiring a new MBA. The results were striking. The facility decision would be made carefully. The organization would use a number of analytical screens, look at the long-term perspective, and amortize the cost over fifteen years. The final decision would be made at a high level and only after input from a number of functions. The hiring decision, on the other hand, would be made at the discretion of the supervisor, with no corporate overview. The time frame would be the present — what the MBA could contribute on day one — and there would be no consideration of any long-term amortization of cost, which would be considerable given the pay, benefits, and office and support costs of a thirty-year-old MBA until age sixty-five. I often also use a follow-on exercise in which managers decide whether to sell a building or lay off employees. After the two exercises, most managers experience varying degrees of the following insights and conclusions:

- Surprise at the true long-term cost of just one employee.

- Concern that there is such a striking difference between the rational decisions made about nonhuman resources and the random decisions made about human resources.

- Agreement that, although the idea of looking at people as long-term investments makes a lot of sense, it would not work in the current organizational environment. (All groups agree on this.)

- A great deal of variance over the option of selling or subleasing a building and letting the employees work at home, where they could still be productive, or laying them off and keeping the building. Interestingly, most top management groups favor getting out of the building, whereas most middle managers say this option would not work because top management would not support it.

The discussion of the different ways decisions are made about people and facilities often focuses on the possibility of organizations' treating people in the same manner as other assets, or human resource accounting. Human resource accounting never really made it into organizational systems in the old paradigm. However, the concept of treating people like other capital assets, conceptualizing them as an investment and amortizing their costs over time, is an excellent way to think in the new paradigm. One of the criticisms of human resource accounting was that it dehumanized people. However, clarity about the true costs and commercial nature of the employment relationship can actually produce a more open and honest relationship.

The Message from the Media

Futurists gain insight into trends and directional shifts by studying and distilling themes from newspapers, magazines, books, and journals. From the mid-eighties on, the popular press has presented overwhelming evidence that we are in the midst of a major paradigm shift. Any content analysis of the press gives a clear indication of a deep and profound change. The fact that the data continue to scream out at us undiminished from the daily newspaper only underscores the velocity of that change.

In 1987, Jerry Flint captured what continues to be a trend when he wrote that "hardly a day goes by without a headline on some major bloodletting: AT&T to cut its payroll by 27,000; IBM letting go 10,000; GM chopping 29,000; United Technologies cutting 11,000; a merged Burroughs/Sperry (UNISYS) 10,000; Eastern Airlines another 1,500; Illinois Central another 1,500; Wang, Tenneco, RCA, Exxon, ALCOA, why go on? The list seemingly never stops" (p. 38).

Today the list still has not stopped! It has accelerated, cutting wider and deeper. Even such staunchly non-layoff organizations as IBM have reversed decades of strong cultural norms and are now laying off employees. The scope of reductions is staggering.

- Two million jobs were eliminated in the 1980s, one million of them in middle management. Half of the 1980 Fortune 500 are missing from the 1990 list (Marks, 1991a).

- "More than eighty-five percent of the Fortune 1000 firms . . . downsized their white collar work force between 1987 and 1991. Almost a million American managers with salaries exceeding $40,000 lost their jobs [in

1990]. Between one and two million pink slips have been handed out each year [from 1988 to 1990]" (Cameron, Freeman, and Mishra, 1991, p. 58).

As the paradigm shift continues, the press also gives us glimpses of a related value shift among some organizational leaders. Steven Prokesch (1987), in a chronicle of what he calls the new creed of "ruthless management that puts corporate survival above all else," writes, "The new order eschews loyalty to workers, products, corporate structure, businesses, communities, even the nation. All such allegiances are viewed as expendable under the new rules. With survival at stake, only market leadership, strong profits, and a high stock price can be allowed to matter" (p. 1).

Prokesch also reports the comments of business leaders such as Gulf and Western's Martin Davis, who says, "You can't be emotionally bound to any particular asset," and Eaton's Stephen Hardis, who sees business as combat and says, "We're more like wartime leaders, in that all we can promise [employees] is blood, sweat and tears" (Prokesch, 1987, p. 8).

Leaders heading those organizations once credited with demonstrating "transformational leadership" (Chrysler, GM, Burroughs, Honeywell) all had a strategy of helping the transformation by major layoffs. At Chrysler, for example, twenty thousand white-collar positions and more than forty-thousand blue-collar jobs were eliminated in the initial "transformation." At the top of the organization, Lee Iacocca reduced his staff by thirty-five vice presidents (Tichy and Devanna, 1986). Flint's description of Chrysler (1987) shows a battle-weary army of survivors rather than a transformed organization. He quotes former Chrysler Chairman Lee Iaccoca: "When we finally held the victory parade, a lot of our soldiers were missing. A lot of people — blue collar, white collar, and dealers — who had been with us in 1979 were no longer around to enjoy the fruits of victory" (p. 38).

Flint also shows the potential for layoff survivor sickness when he writes of the "dark side" of efficiency: "The blood

bath of firing goes on. That's the dark side of the current improvement in corporate efficiency. . . . After all, those workers from the production line now laid off, and those middle
managers now adrift didn't hire themselves. They didn't create bureaucratic bloat. They didn't make the foolish acquisitions, or product choices. . . . In all of this, business is building up a good deal of resentment that will one day come to
haunt it" (p. 38).

FROM NURTURING TO
VIOLENCE: THE SYMBOLISM
OF LAYOFF LANGUAGE

The symbolism of layoff language patterns provides powerful evidence of a paradigm shift. For example, a few years
ago, a manager investigated the language patterns in her own
layoff environment.

Semantic Sensing

Sally, a human resource manager, was convinced that "no one
[was] talking about development" anymore in her organization after layoffs were planned. She and I decided to test that
feeling. For two weeks, Sally kept track of both "nurturing"
and "violent" phrases. She jotted them down during group
meetings, and after one-on-one meetings. She captured hall-
way talk during a half-day top management planning meeting. The outcome? Violent terminology won hands down!
While this in itself was not surprising (the organization was
intensely engaged in layoff planning), what was interesting
was the size of the victory. For all the human resource group
meetings, there were only four "nurturing" entries as opposed
to over twenty "violent" entries, yet this was an organization
with a long tradition of training and development and a strong
and professional human resource staff. Violent words such
as *take out*, *kill*, *shoot*, and *terminate* outscored helping words

such as *develop, grow,* and *train* by about three to one. Although we used a simple sensing process rather than a sophisticated scientific study, the results were nonetheless illuminating. When they were fed back to a human resources committee, the consensus was that violent words had markedly increased over the past few years and that ten years ago, the group would have had "an opposite outcome."

I have since asked small groups of managers planning post-layoff revitalization efforts to come up with words and phrases that described the way they wanted to relate to their employees. Although the small-group results were not as spectacular as the two-week study, the managers were surprised at the language patterns that had emerged within their organizations, particularly when these patterns were contrasted with the managers' intentions. During one session, a vice president turned to a comptroller and said, "The last time I came for an increase in my R&D budget, you asked me 'How many have you shot?' As if I had to pay for my new product development with the blood of employees!"

The Language of Layoffs
as the Language of Assassination

Clinical behavioral practitioners have always carefully examined and given credence to the symbolism of communication patterns. Leaders struggling to revitalize organizations should do the same. Robert Marshak and Judith Katz (1992, p. 2) provide a good guideline for leaders when they say, "Explore literal messages symbolically, and symbolic messages literally," because "when symbolic communications are looked at, or listened to, for their literal as well as symbolic meaning a wider range of diagnostic speculation and/or inquiry is revealed." If leaders follow this guideline and understand the language of violence literally, they can see that managers who are "taking out" or "terminating" their fellow employees see themselves, at some level, as doing severe harm to others. Consequently these managers experience anger and survivor guilt.

It is neither a coincidence nor a matter to be lightly dismissed that the language of layoffs is the language of assassination.

Language as a Safe Abstraction

Individuals also use symbolism to distance or somehow abstract themselves from the pain or embarrassment of reality. We have spawned a number of euphemisms for the act of separating people involuntarily from their jobs. It is easier for top executives to talk to bankers and security analysts about "restructuring" than to production workers about "termination." "Downsizing" feels better than "reduction-in-force," and "rightsizing" has an almost moral ring to it. Organizational leaders' invention of "safe" words is a clue to their repressed feelings and a window on their own survivor sickness.

FROM LONG TERM TO SHORT TERM: THE SHRINKING PLANNING HORIZON

Another harbinger of the new paradigm is the shrinking time frame that organizations apply to almost everything. Organizations are reducing cycle time, planning time, budgeting time, travel time, development time, and significantly, employee tenure time.

The Just-in-Time Employee

Stimulated by the current frenzy, driven primarily by security analysts, to make short-term (sometimes less than quarterly) incremental profit gains, many organizations find that their strategic horizon has been drastically shortened. In one organization, the so-called long-range strategic plan is now an eighteen-month document, and even that time period seems contrived and artificial to those who are involved in leading and managing the organization. Employees too are affected by the short-term frenzy. Their long-term careers have become short-term jobs. In the new reality, people are becoming task-specific disposable components of a system that is already short term, and getting shorter. We are approaching the era of the *just-in-time employee.* The increasing number of temporary help agencies offering both clerical and professional employees, a growing contract employee industry, and a marked increase in employee classifications such as part-time, temporary, permanent part-time, and on-call testifies to the changing paradigm.

Bait and Switch Time Victims

Employees who accepted jobs under the old employment contract but are now ruled by the new may feel that they are victims of a type of bait and switch operation, because the ground rules have been changed in the middle of the game. When they joined, they expected a long-term relationship. Their tenure was often rewarded by periodic celebrations and organizational trinkets such as tie bars, earrings, key chains, and wall plaques. Now, under the new contract, leaving is more often the desired outcome.

FROM SYNERGISTIC TO REDUCTIONISTIC: TAKING APART IS BETTER THAN PUTTING TOGETHER

Synergy is an old-paradigm word. Once, organizations added components, built themselves up, developed people for the long term, and a form of magic happened: two and two came out to more than four. No longer. The new paradigm is reductionistic. The shift in preference is from large to small. In human resource terms, the shift is from long-term employee development to short-term employee fit.

When Big Was Better

In the era after World War II, big was in. The United States had won the war by mobilizing large hierarchical organizations. What was good for General Motors truly was perceived as good for everyone. Books such as *The Man in the Gray Flannel Suit* (1955) and *The Organization Man* (1956) provide a window on the work ethic and organizational culture of the time. Large, hierarchical, bureaucratic, male-dominated ("man" was appropriate in the book titles) organizations were the norm. Many organizations indexed the importance of managerial jobs by the number of people supervised. Job evaluation systems were developed that gave great weight to this span-of-control factor. Many of these organization systems are in use within organizations that now value downsizing. Organizations that valued size also tended to value development. The party line was, "My primary job is developing people." The refrain toward the top of the organization was, "I can't go anywhere until I develop a replacement." The assumption was growth, the pay-off was promotion, and the currency of the realm was size. Contrast that paradigm with today's reality, when the assumption is quarter-to-quarter bottom-line growth, the pay-off is that you get to keep your job and do it again next quarter, and the currency of the realm is getting the job done with a smaller, more flexible organization.

An Executive's New Reality

Robert once headed a large division of an organization attempting to rebound from layoffs triggered by a merger. After he too was laid off he said, "I used to get kudos for hiring and developing people — used to give them myself to my people. That was the pay-off, growing people, running big organizations. Now [the board of directors] gives [the CEO] big raises, stock, every other damn thing for cutting back, for taking people out. The headhunters that call don't care about who I mentored — the money I spent on training. They want to know how I did more with less."

LAYOFF SURVIVOR SICKNESS: THE LEGACY

The reality of the paradigm shift is becoming increasingly clear, and we can only live in one paradigm — we can't go back. What we can do, what we must do, if we are to revitalize our organizations, is to deal with layoff survivor sickness, the legacy of the demise of the old paradigm and the old employment contract.

In an internal AT&T memo, Joel Moses (1987) provides a clear articulation of this bitter legacy:

> We have very "disturbed" managers. Managers who are forced to make work force reduction decisions without any guidance, training, or support are becoming cynical. Or those who really care are being torn apart when making decisions that they are unprepared to make.
>
> Open hostility is surfacing as never before and its focus is toward the company rather than toward the competition or the marketplace where such energies can be productively channeled.
>
> The amount of suppressed, covert hostility lurking just below the surface in many people is truly frightening. Unfortunately, much of the frustration, anger, and depression is taking its toll on the non-work lives of our people.
>
> Frequently, its manifestations are deteriorating physical and psychological health. The impact on managers' health in the future can't be ignored and may be approaching crisis proportions.
>
> At the same time, we have noted a marked increase in symptoms of depression among managers we have studied. Today's survivors are often disillusioned, frustrated, bitter, and, most of all, lacking in hope.
>
> One can't help wondering what kinds of managers they will be like in the future as they populate senior levels at AT&T (pp. 35-36).

Jeffrey Hallett (1987) calls for us in the United States to adopt a new perspective, new "worklife visions." He argues that the United States "has long since lost the position of economic, political, and technological predominance that we held for so much of the 20th century" (p. 58). His prescription for dealing with survivor sickness includes "self-reliance," a theme that will be discussed in later chapters. Hallett says that organizations should "never, never say to an employee that the job is steady, guaranteed long-term, permanent or safe." Instead, Hallett suggests that self-reliance can become "a powerful statement about or expectation regarding work and society. The concept connotes a complete reversal of the fundamental notion that we 'work' for someone else. Instead, it says we work only for ourselves, that we take the responsibility for our own performance and progress, that we take responsibility for our own futures, and that we have the knowledge and the capabilities necessary for success" (p. 62).

LEARNINGS AND IMPLICATIONS

We are experiencing four dimensions of a basic shift in the relationship between people and organizations. Insights into this paradigm shift are found in organizational assumptions about the purpose of people (from assets to be grown and nurtured to costs to be cut); the symbolism of organizational language (from nurturing to violent); organizational time horizons (from long-term career development to short-term job fit and short-term profit orientation); and organizational preferences (from building up to taking apart). The legacy of these profound changes is often an embittered work force and reduced productivity at a time when organizations most need an optimistic work force and high productivity.

This is a no-fault, long-term change. There are no "good" people and "bad" people. Managers did not make the paradigm shift happen or set out to trade off people for cost reduction.

All levels of employees — top executives, middle managers, first-level supervisors, exempt and nonexempt employees — are in the same boat, part of the same uncomfortable, often painful, cultural voyage. Nevertheless, people tend to blame others — usually the next person up on the organization chart — for what is a basic systemic change, beyond anyone's control. This survivor blaming phenomenon, described in more detail in Chapter Four, is not a productive way to deal with the fundamental change facing individuals and organizations.

Those occupying leadership roles are key to the survival of organizations and the rekindling of the spirit and creativity of the work force. The new challenge to leaders is much more complex and stressful than operating within the predictability of the old paradigm. Both organizational leaders struggling to compete in a global marketplace and individuals seeking relevance in a time of change must first learn to let go of the comfort of the predictable past. This is not a simple intellectual or rational decision. It involves struggling with the same inner demons that have confronted survivors of other forms of trauma. This struggle is the topic of the next chapter.

Part Two

The

Survivor

Experience

3

Learning from the Past:
The Survivor Syndrome
Across Time

"I didn't realize that I was probably suffering
from some form of depression, but it was
going on, and on, and on. I mean day after
day, feeling the same way."

A general manager once asked
for help with what he saw as the "short-term motivation problems" of the layoff survivors in his organization. He wanted
to get on with business and thought a one-shot external intervention would do the job. Unfortunately, his diagnosis of
the depth and staying power of layoff-survivor symptoms was
wrong. You do not "fix" survivors as you do a leaky faucet
by calling in a specialist for a mechanical repair. As I show
later in this book, a true fix requires a "culture-busting" change
for both individuals and their organizations.

In the confusion of the post-layoff environment, it is easy

for managers to underestimate the severity of survivor symptoms, both in those they manage and in themselves. However, layoff survivors suffer long-lasting symptoms that are in
many ways similar to the symptoms of other survivors. An
awareness of these similarities not only defines the seriousness of layoff survivor sickness but also stimulates the emotional release and grieving that must take place before organizations and survivors can move forward. The example of
the Gunslinger shows how a deeper understanding of universal survivor symptoms can unblock organizational denial.

THE GUNSLINGER'S
TASK FORCE

The CEO of a regional financial services organization had
gone outside and hired a new chief operating officer who had
a reputation as a turnaround expert. His most common nick-
name was the Gunslinger, but later in his reign, because he
made quick decisions without adequate data, he was also
called No Toes. Figuratively speaking, he would fire his gun
before pulling it from its holster, blowing off his toes. The
bank was in bad shape when he came in. It was internally
focused, fat, and overbureaucratized. If ever an organization
needed downsizing, this one did, and the Gunslinger was only
too happy to oblige. He initiated a series of rapid and substantial layoffs, at times eliminating entire functions. He followed up with a requirement that each remaining department
"totem pole" its employees and terminate the bottom 10 percent. There is nothing wrong with reducing the staff of a fat
and marginally productive organization. Laying off a large
number of middle managers can eliminate bureaucratic bot-
tlenecks and facilitate communications. The process of totem
poling can also lead to the establishment of objective performance standards. The reason these results did not appear in
the Gunslinger's bank was that the changes were accom-

plished through a bad process. There was no concern with how the reductions were made, and survivor feelings were repressed and denied. A bad process was then compounded by the organizational culture. For thirty years the bank had valued tenure and emphasized loyalty. Its culture was accurately described by one long-term employee as "low pay, low stress, high security"! When this old-paradigm organization tried to become a new-paradigm organization through an ineffective process, the basic bind came into operation, and the organization was paralyzed with survivor sickness.

A courageous vice president of computer operations, who worked for the Gunslinger, formed a cross-functional task force, despite the lack of any real support from his boss, in an attempt to get things moving again. The group, made up of eight upper-middle managers from across the organization, asked me to help them, but after a few meetings, it was apparent that they were going in circles. They would discuss in weighty intellectual terms the way that the past layoffs and future uncertainty had paralyzed the organization, nod their heads, and look to me for suggestions. When I would ask them to talk about their own feelings they would either talk about their pain with calm, nonpainful affect or talk about others' feelings.

A behavior common to layoff survivors was taking place. They were denying the personal emotional impact of the reductions and consequently blocking the necessary catharsis and grieving. Before this task force could do much for their organization they had to recognize and deal with their own survivor issues. However, talking about feelings and emotions was never a part of the bank's culture, and with the Gunslinger still the top decision maker in the organization and in charge of their fates, wondering what they were up to, this task force was particularly resistant to experimental behavior.

In order to try to break the circular process, it was decided to meet outside the office and for a longer period than their normal two-hour meeting. We met at a conference center, starting after lunch and continuing well into the evening.

What took place then was one of those special times in group dynamics that can neither be predicted nor artificially recreated. I offer it here to illustrate the importance of overcoming denial, not to suggest that this particular intervention be routinely applied. The process we went through had four steps:

■ After some general relaxing and centering exercises, which helped each person to feel more at ease and in touch with their individual boundaries, each group member was asked to think of a major survival situation that he or she, or someone he or she knew, had experienced. With the exception of layoffs, all survival situations were fair game. What came out were events such as car crashes, divorces, and unexpected deaths. After individually fixing a chosen event in their minds and reexperiencing the feelings, the task force members wrote down the feelings.

■ The participants were invited, still working alone, to think of a major survivor event to which they could relate but that they had not experienced. Examples of what they came up with were surviving a plane crash, a POW experience, and a potentially fatal illness. Again, they were asked to put themselves in the survivor's position and write out their feelings.

■ The participants shared the events and their feelings. It soon became clear that their feelings for both the real and the fantasized events were similar. They had experienced fear, anger, depression, and anxiety, all grounded in a core sense of violation.

■ The task force members fantasized further survivor situations and collectively used them as metaphors for layoff situations. What they came up with was powerful: they were travelers over Donner Pass, staying alive through the winter by cannibalizing their fellow travellers; they were in charge of life rafts and had to decide who could stay and who had to be thrown overboard;

they were soldiers parachuted into hostile territory and abandoned while their generals took early retirement and forgot about them. Metaphors like these flowed uninterrupted for almost an hour and did the most to help the group understand the depth of survivor symptoms.

It was an emotional session, and it served to break patterns of denial by dramatizing the shared sense of violation the task force members felt. The insight helped them draft practical programs to deal with the way layoffs took place in their organization and to facilitate the necessary grieving and emotional release for those who remained.

This intervention also illustrates the situational and unpredictable nature of intervention techniques. I have subsequently attempted to duplicate this process with spectacularly bad results. It not only has not worked, but in one case, it offended and set back the group. Intervention success seems to be a function of the skill of the facilitator, the stage of the group, the level of trust, the culture of the organization, the emotional authenticity of the group, and a number of other factors, not all of which are yet understood even by trained facilitators. The intervention example used here is not meant to be a recipe but only to provide one example of the rich variety of exercises that can be used to get survivors in touch with and to clarify their emotions. I have found the metaphor of the surviving children discussed in Chapter One to be a more consistently reliable tool than the process illustrated here. The lesson in this for managers is that there is no single recipe for a successful intervention and that good diagnosis is essential.

Also, the intervention's positive results probably would not have happened if the Gunslinger had remained at the bank, but a few months after the breakthrough session, he left. The story in the hallways was that, like his Old West counterparts, he outwore his welcome. The chairman, like an Old West town mayor, had hired the Gunslinger to rid the town of bandits, the fat, over-bureaucratized organization. The

Gunslinger did clean out the bandits, but then he stayed on and became a bigger problem than the bandits. He had fixed one problem but had to leave before the wounds he had created in the process could heal.

THE GUNSLINGER'S
TASK FORCE LEARNINGS

- It is easy to underestimate the depth and tenacity of layoff survivor feelings.

- In the heat of battle, with change, confusion, and uncertainty swirling throughout the organization, it is easy, and often seems safer, to block and deny survivor feelings.

- Understanding, both in your head and your heart, that the feelings of layoff survivors and those who have survived other forms of trauma are connected is an effective means of getting past blockage and denial.

- Those attempting to help others deal with survivor issues must first work on their own feelings.

SURVIVOR LINKAGES

All those involved in layoffs should broaden their cognitive and emotional (head and heart) understanding of the linkages among survivors of trauma. This broad understanding is necessary if managers in particular are to heal themselves and then help others. I will use powerful well-known historical examples of survivorship to define survivor linkages. In comparing layoff survivors to survivors of much more life-threatening events, I do not intend to trivialize or dilute the pain and horror that these other survivors endured. Nor am I equating the violation experienced by a layoff survivor with, for example, that experienced by a Nazi concentration camp survivor. The difference in magnitude is immeasurable. That is not to say, however, that layoff survivors do not experience violation. The forty-six-year-old middle manager who joined an organization as a new college graduate, has been conditioned into relying on the organization to meet his social, financial, and self-esteem needs, but wakes up one morning in midcareer to find that the organization can no longer honor its end of the psychological employment contract does experience violation. His sense of personal relevance and value has been taken away. When a single survivor understands that all survivors share the same emotions, even though in greatly varying degrees, he or she gains head, and more importantly, heart insight into both the seriousness and the normalcy of these emotions.

There are three primary linkages: (1) similar symptoms, (2) a common sense of violation and a preoccupation with death imagery, and (3) blurred distinctions between those who do and those who do not survive and a shared sense of victimization among victims and victimizers. I will summarize the findings in each area before looking at the significant details.

Similarity of Symptoms

After the space shuttle *Challenger* disaster, the thousands of people who had worked in the shuttle program felt like disaster survivors. Descriptions of the symptoms experienced by these survivors and by layoff survivors at Occidental Petroleum provide an example of survivor symptom similarity. Shortly after the disaster, observers said that the shuttle survivors experienced "guilt, anxiety, and fear," with the full intensity of these feelings yet to be dealt with because of "denial" (Schwadel, Moffett, Harris, and Lowenstein, 1986, p. 27). Very similar words were used by human resource consultant Marshall Stelifox when he described the symptoms of "anxiety, distrust, fear, and insecurity" among survivors at Occidental

Petroleum (Fowler, 1986, p. 23). Stelifox may also have been the first to use the term *survivors' syndrome.*

Preoccupation with Violation

Robert Lifton (1967) analyzed the survivors of the Hiroshima atomic bomb and found they had a fixation with "death imagery." He also found that a preoccupation with images of death and destruction is common among survivors of other traumatic situations. While I have not witnessed a fixation with death imagery among layoff survivors, both symbolic and literal descriptions of violation and destruction can be found in the direct quotations from layoff survivors presented in Chapters Four and Five.

I have also found gallows humor common among layoff survivors. At one level, this is a form of comic relief. At a symbolic level, it is also a variant on survivors' unconscious use of death imagery. An example of the ease with which violent imagery is integrated into day-to-day layoff discussions is the personnel manager who attended a meeting on the administrative aspects of implementing an impending layoff, and afterward said in an offhand way that she felt she had just attended a Nazi staff meeting in which the number of Jews who could fit in a boxcar was "rationally" decided. These extreme images of destruction are common among those who process layoff victims out the door, and the ease with which this personnel manager conjured up this horrible image is evidence that a survivor connection was percolating in her unconscious while she sat through that meeting.

Victims and Perpetrators Feel Victimized

The metaphor of the surviving children often leads managers to the conclusion that those who make layoff decisions, other layoff survivors, and the layoff victims are all in the same funk. In non-layoff survivor situations, survivors, at least, share similar feelings of guilt, and often similar feelings of depression.

COLLUSION, DEPRESSION, AND COURAGE

Jerry Harvey is the inventor of the well-known Abilene Paradox, a parable that describes how people collude collectively to do things they do not want to do individually. Harvey, using the genre of a Calvinistic preacher, wrote two "sermons": "Eichmann in the Organization" (1985a), and "Getting Eichmann Out of the Organization" (1985b). Although these have since been somewhat revised for publication (Harvey, 1988), I find the unpublished versions more powerful because they seem less sanitized.

I have used Harvey's Eichmann sermons when working with "flat" groups, ones that do not show much emotion or passion. Whether they become angry or agree with Harvey's themes, the groups usually open up during the discussion and learn a broader frame of reference for understanding survivors' feelings. Although I have sometimes supplied the sermons in advance of a meeting, my preferred method is to drop them on a group cold, have people read them to themselves, and then open the floor for discussion and reaction. That way, people do not come into the meeting with their defenses up.

Harvey summarizes his major themes when he writes of "organizational seduction and rape" (OSR):

> The basic theme of the sermon is that selectively firing or laying off people from organizations for reasons of economy is an act of organizational seduction and rape. Furthermore, the roles and thought patterns required to carry out that form of seduction and rape are identical to the roles and thought patterns which were required to conduct the holocaust. . . . The second theme is equally unattractive. It is that those whom we identify as victims of OSR and those whom we identify as victimizers, must think and behave in an identical fashion. . . . A third theme is that we could create other ways of thinking

and behaving which are not only organizationally productive, but also are respectful of our deepest yearnings
to treat one another with kindness, decency, and . . .
love (1985a, pp. 1–2).

Harvey perceives survivor sickness as a dulling of our
"moral sensibilities," which "decreases the probability of our
individual and collective survival" (1985a, p. 41). He also
describes it as "marasmus." Derived from the Greek, marasmus
means "'to waste away.' It generally refers to the progressive
emaciation which occurs in infants when they are denied the
loving care of an adult. It is caused by 'anaclitic depression,'
which, in turn, means depression which is induced by being
separated from someone you love or care for or need" (1981,
p. 1).

Wasting away — mental and emotional withdrawal and
loss of affect — due to depression is a symptom experienced
by survivors and victims. Most managers who work in organizations hit hard by layoffs have had experience with organizational units where marasmus seems to be the operant
word. The survivors do seem to be wasting away. In Harvey's
model, the irrevocable outcome of unchecked marasmus is
death for the organization and, at the least, what Richard
Leider (1992) calls "inner-kill" for the individual.

The behavior of declining organizations that Uri Merry
and George Brown describe in *The Neurotic Behavior of Organizations* (1987) also is found in organizations suffering from
marasmus. The characteristics are:

- Negative self-image; failure script of organization [a negative self-fulfilling prophecy].

- Energy down; organization pervaded by low motivation,
  frustration, unhappiness, boredom, and hopelessness.

- Disagreement on goals and values throughout organization; norm disruptment with extreme deviations; organized life loses meaning.

- High magnitude of dysfunctioning, lack of reserve resources, failure of self-image, and fear of letting go make
   change extremely difficult; rational organizational development methods give no results (pp. 44–45).

Fania Fenelon was a survivor of the Nazis' Birkenau ex-
termination camp. In her book *Playing for Time* (1977), she
shared her experiences as a member of the camp orchestra.
The group played and sang for their captors and thus survived the death surrounding them. Fenelon says it took her
a long time to deal with her survivor sickness: "After 30 years
of silence during which I tried to forget the unforgettable,
I saw that it was impossible. What I had to do was exorcise
the orchestra" (p. 1). In other words, she could not escape from
the memory; she had to come to terms with it.

She wrote of meeting another prisoner — one who would
be a victim — in a field: "Of course we met other prisoners;
they stared after us, disgusted, poised for insult. Yet one of
them smiled at me. She held out her arms and I gave her my
bunch of flowers. Incredulous, she stared at her hand where
the blue Hari Bills quivered, closed her fingers over them, and
ran off" (p. 202).

Fenelon's image, conjured up through the guilt and repression of thirty years, stimulated another in me. It was of
a group of managers buying a farewell drink for a recently laid-
off, long-term colleague. The group shared a drink, and then
the laid-off manager abruptly stopped the conversation, put
his glass down, and hurried away, leaving the group in silence.

Harvey (1988, p. 76) writes what he calls an "old parable" to illustrate his perception of the consequences of the
decision to participate — he would say collude — in any coer-
cive system, regardless of severity. In this parable, he describes
a man attempting to "engage the services of a woman of the
night. In the negotiation process he offered her $5.00. In a
fury, she shouted, "Five dollars! What do you think I am?'
'That, Madame,' he replied, 'has already been established. All
we are doing now is debating the price.'"

Harvey raises some hard philosophical questions for organizational leaders. What was the price that was paid by the survivors that evening in the bar, and were they, in their own way, "playing for time?" Does the decision to participate (collude?) in an economic system anchored in a philosophy of layoffs always demand payment in the form of layoff survivor sickness? Harvey would offer an affirmative response to these questions: the decision to collude in a layoff causes depression which, left unchecked, causes marasmus, which, in turn, leads to symbolic or literal death. The cure, to Harvey, demands two acts of courage; refusing to participate and confronting and exploring ethical and moral issues in organizations. He uses the example of the Danes' refusal to cooperate with Nazi demands to turn over Danish Jews as an example of this kind of courage.

My answer is that layoffs are an inevitable consequence of new and long-term economic and social forces. No one is at fault and a personal decision not to participate is not a realistic solution. I agree with Harvey that courage is a key factor, but the kind of courage managers need is not the courage to resist, but rather the courage to participate and end the problems that leave survivors feeling as if they had colluded. As I will discuss in future chapters, making a difference involves living and managing in paradox and confusion and acquiring new skills that are relevant to the new employment contract.

LIFTON'S MODEL OF HIROSHIMA ATOMIC BOMB SURVIVORS

An illuminating way of viewing the universality of survivorship is through the symbolic lenses of psychiatry. Robert Lifton's (1967) psychological analysis of Hiroshima atomic bomb survivors created a model that can be applied to all survivor situations. The left-hand column of the list on p. 46

shows the themes Lifton found in the survivors of Hiroshima as these themes are manifested in both Hiroshima and death camp survivors. The right-hand column shows my interpretation of these themes in layoff survivors.

Death Imprint

In Lifton's terminology, a *death imprint* is the initial violation. In Hiroshima the triggering event was the bombing; in organizations it is the layoffs. This event starts the chain of emotional response. Death imprinting causes mourning for the way things were, "for beliefs that have been shattered" (Lifton, 1967, p. 484).

Although there is an immense difference between the horror and fear faced by Hiroshima survivors and the disruption and uncertainty faced by those who remain in organizations after reductions, layoff survivors are imprinted by the layoffs. They do mourn the way things were—the good old-paradigm days that have been destroyed. When survivors wish former bosses were still in charge, because they wouldn't let this happen, or when they lament the loss of an organization's founder, because he would run the company better, the survivors are looking back, searching for beliefs that have been shattered.

A death imprint has three subprocesses: symbolic reactivation, world destruction imagery, and psychic mutation. Lifton found that symbolic reactivation occurred for Hiroshima survivors when they saw media reports of atomic deaths or were reminded of their survivorship through events like an annual commemorative ceremony. Organizational parallels occur when each succeeding wave of layoffs reminds survivors of their status. Reactivation triggers symptoms of guilt, fear, and anxiety. It also makes layoff survivors feel paranoid, inauthentic, and disinclined to take risks. Although layoff survivors do not envision their "ultimate death," newspaper and television reports of bad economic conditions, layoffs, divestitures, and mergers encourage a form of world destruction

Hiroshima and Death Camp Survivors	Layoff Survivors
Death imprint The bombing.	Death imprint The layoffs.
Symbolic reactivation News reports of atomic deaths. Annual August 6 ceremony.	Symbolic reactivation News reports of mergers, layoffs, and acquisitions. Empty offices, vacant parking slots.
World destruction imagery Visions of "ultimate death, ultimate separation."	World destruction imagery Projections of failure of capitalistic system.
Psychic mutation Altered perception of reality—"coping mechanisms" necessary to survive death camps.	Psychic mutation Joy in work, spontaneity, and creative energy no longer part of reality.
Death guilt Resentment toward those who died.	Death guilt Guilt feelings associated with luck—being in the right place at the right time. Feeling that those who left escaped the consequences of survivorship.
Psychic numbing Perception of oneself as an object—"These dreadful, degrading things are not happening to me."	Psychic numbing Process of denial—"That's the way it is in business organizations."
Miscarried repair "Musselmanner" behavior. Vitality is perceived as immoral.	Miscarried repair Lack of risk taking; going through the motions. Vitality perceived as immoral.

Victim bonding and suspicion	Victim bonding and suspicion
Resentment by Hiroshima survivors toward Bikini atoll survivors.	Resentment by line personnel toward staff personnel.
Delayed paranoia.	Survivor status hidden at outside social gatherings.
Formulation	Formulation
"Establish new internal and external relationships."	Break organizational codependence.

imagery among those survivors. In some old-paradigm organizations with a history of paternalism, layoffs trigger such a deep erosion of trust that survivors question whether any for-profit organization can survive with, as they see it, the permanent loss of motivation and commitment.

Psychic mutation describes the altered perception of reality that individuals succumb to in order to get through terrible events. It is a process of numbing one's feelings and blocking our previous ideas of the way things ought to be. Death camp prisoners developed a type of apathy, make-it-through-one-day-at-a-time resignation and a type of acceptance that the horror of their environment was "normal." Long-term layoff survivors also undergo a form of psychic mutation. They often accept fear and anxiety, and just try to make it through the day. It is as though creative energy, spontaneity, and joy in work are not part of reality.

Death Guilt

A number of mental health professionals believe that all deaths cause guilt in those who survive. Deep and often unexpressed or not understood feelings of resentment at being abandoned lead to this survivor guilt. Hiroshima survivors suffered from survivor guilt directly attributable to the deaths caused by the atomic bomb. The work of Brockner and others (1985, 1986) gives evidence that a form of survivor guilt exists in layoff situations even though no literal deaths are involved.

Layoff survivors who feel "depressed" or "saddened" by empty offices, or, in the case of one person, by all the extra parking slots in the executive parking garage, are manifesting survivor guilt, triggered by a form of symbolic reactivation.

Psychic Numbing

In Lifton's study, psychic numbing not only occurred immediately following the survivor experience, it dominated the survivors' entire life-style. Numbing begins with denial: "The survivor's major defense is the cessation of feeling" (Lifton, p. 500).

As an example of psychic numbing, Lifton cites the behavior of the people referred to in some concentration camps as "musselmänner." (This term grew out of erroneous perception of a Muslim coping mechanism.) Lifton quotes the following description of the psychic numbing of musselmänner prisoners from Primo Levi's *Survival in Auschwitz*. It is similar to the condition Harvey calls marasmus. "The musselmänner, the drowned, form the backbone of the camp, an anonymous mass, continually renewed and always identical, of non-men who march and labor in silence, the spark dead within them, already too empty to really suffer, one hesitates to call them living: one hesitates to call their death death, in the face of which they have no fear, as they are too tired to understand." (p. 502)

Miscarried Repair

The ultimate effect of psychic numbing is *miscarried repair,* which is analogous to an overreaction of the body's immune system. The defenses against infection become a noxious force. In Hiroshima survivors, miscarried repair took the form of complaints of fatigue and other bodily complaints. Lifton observes that these survivors' "numbing is such that vitality is perceived as immoral" (p. 503).

Layoff survivors are seen as flat, tired, and risk averse. Being "up" and positive often seems countercultural. Hunkering in the trenches, not taking risks, and keeping a tight rein on emotions that need airing are defensive reactions that are neither healthy for the individual nor productive for the organization. This defensiveness, or miscarried repair, causes layoff survivors too to perceive vitality as immoral.

Victim Bonding and Suspicion

Survivors often have difficulty establishing authentic relationships with others for two reasons. First, they are invested in a victim identity. They are survivor-victims. Second, they are suspicious of others. This suspicion can turn into a form of "delayed paranoia." Hiroshima survivors have "a group tie built around common victimization. . . . The survivor feels drawn into permanent union with the force that killed so many others around him. His guilt is intensified as is his sense that his own life is counterfeit" (Lifton, 1967, p. 511). Identity as a survivor can lead to rivalry with other survivors. The Hiroshima survivors, for example, resented the attention given to the survivors of the 1954 Bikini atoll hydrogen bomb fallout. Layoff survivors continually index the severity and ruthlessness of the layoffs in their organization against that of other organizations. Another prevalent index of severity is the line-staff, headquarters-field, or top-bottom balance. Line units will lament that they "took harder hits" than staff units, saying, "after all, we bring in the revenue." Field units resent layoff leniency in headquarters units, and lower levels resent the top management not taking its fair share. And so it goes; all units are invested in their I'm-a-bigger-victim-than-you syndrome.

Survivors are suspicious of others. One form this suspicion takes in layoffs is the survivor blaming phenomenon: everyone blames everyone else. The Hiroshima survivors turned inward and clung to their victim identity. As both types of survivors struggle over time with repressed rage, their isolation and suspicion is reinforced by what Lifton describes as others' contagion anxiety: "The essence of contagion anxiety is, if I touch him, or come too close, I will experience his death and his annihilation. Hence the universal tendency to honor martyrs and reject survivors" (p. 518). Survivors in organizations known to be going through severe layoffs often worry about how their outside contacts are affected by this knowledge. Some layoff survivors say that they do not own up to their place of employment when they attend outside social events. Others report limiting their social life and spending more leisure time at home. Contagion anxiety flourishes in many organizations during the awkward time between layoff victims' getting the word and leaving the organization. Survivors are reluctant to engage with these victims. Conversation is stilted or nonexistent, and empathy and concern are often suppressed.

Formulation

Lifton's cure for survivor sickness involves a process of structuring a new relationship with the world and coming to terms with the permanence of loss. He describes how "the dropping of the atomic bomb in Hiroshima annihilated a general sense of life's coherence" among the survivors, and he points out that Freud "described the survivor's need to come to gradual recognition of the new reality, of the world which no longer contains that which has been lost" (p. 525). Similarly, the cure for layoff-survivor sickness requires that survivors accept the "new reality" and let go of the old paradigm. As I will discuss later, the cure demands that survivors muster up the courage to break organizational codependency and live organizational life as adventurers, not victims.

LEARNINGS AND IMPLICATIONS

It is important for those of us who must revitalize ourselves or our organizations to understand the true depth and staying power of survivor symptoms. We can increase both our head and heart understanding by examining the linkages between layoff survivors and survivors of more severe traumas.

I have used the ideas of Jerry Harvey, the psychodynamic theories of Robert Lifton, and a story of survivors confronting their symptoms in order to illustrate the universality of survivor symptoms. Unfortunately, there are countless contemporary examples, including the civilian and military survivors from both sides of the Vietnam War and, more recently, survivors of African famines and of the civil wars in the republics of the former Soviet Union and in Eastern Europe. Another look at survivor symptoms is found in the works of Aleksandr Solzhenitsyn, who writes with a passion fueled by his own survivor sickness. One need only journey with him through the Gulag Archipelago (1974), or spend a day with him examining the marasmus of Ivan Denisovich (1963), to visualize the specter of a gulag of organizations, populated by demoralized employees with spirits atrophied by a plague of survivor sickness.

My primary purpose in this chapter was to broaden managers' understanding of survivorship and set the stage to analyze layoff survivor sickness through the literal and symbolic descriptions of survivors' feelings in the survivors' own words. As I listen to these survivors, it often seems to me that the voices of many earlier survivors have reached across time and mingled with those of the layoff survivors to reflect the universality of survivor feelings.

4

Speaking for Themselves:
Layoff Survivor Stories

"There is a sense that you have done
something wrong if you get laid off. I don't
think anyone escapes that. Even if, in their
rational minds, they say, 'I was good, it just
happened to be the job I was in.' There's
something down deep that says, 'You weren't
good enough, there's something wrong, you
pissed somebody off, you didn't play the game.'"

With a few exceptions, most of
the research on the effects of layoffs on survivors is limited
by its laboratory orientation. Although valuable, it has not captured the gut-wrenching trauma or plumbed the true emotional depth of layoff survivor sickness. To allow the reader
to experience the turmoil and anger of survivors, this chapter and the next report on a field study of real survivors in
an existing organization. These chapters consist mainly of
direct quotes from the survivors, to provide the reader with
a personal, undiluted feel for the true emotions and thoughts
of layoff survivors. The universal survivor feelings explored in

Chapter Three and the pain of living through the transition to the new paradigm described in Chapter Two can be found in the voices of these survivors. The intervention strategies I will describe later also build upon the foundation of personal understanding developed in this and the next chapter. I encourage you to go with the flow; allow yourself to be flooded by the layoff survivors' feelings and perceptions. For those preferring a different journey, the quotations are organized by theme and therefore may be read selectively.

ORGANIZATIONAL CHARACTERISTICS

The study took place in a large multinational firm headquartered on the East Coast. At the time of the initial study (1987), the organization was experiencing financial problems and implementing a downsizing that called for significant across-the-board layoffs. A prototypical old employment contract organization, it had a number of programs to integrate employees into the organization over a long period of time. While there was no formal non-layoff policy, there was a shared expectation that, with acceptable performance, an employee could count on her or his job despite economic conditions.

This organization provided a unique opportunity; it had top managers who were courageous enough to charter the study, ask the hard questions, and contribute to research. It was diverse enough in terms of products, population, and geography for the results to be relevant to other organizations. Since it had a very strong attachment to the old employment contract, the results are also relevant to organizations that are struggling to move away from the old paradigm. In the spirit of "modern" employee relations, the organization had provided support services that promoted employee dependency, and the psychological bond supporting this relationship was seen to be violated when the organization instituted layoffs.

RESEARCH METHODOLOGY

The initial study consisted of two samples: structured interviews of small groups of layoff survivors and individual interviews with human resource professionals involved in layoff administration. A second, more limited follow-up study (discussed in Chapter Five) was conducted five years after the initial study. The initial group interviews involved ten randomly selected groups of eight to fifteen survivors from recent layoffs. These groups represented a variety of businesses and job levels. The interview sessions were taped, and the transcripts were analyzed. (Appendix A provides additional information on the interview methodology and group demographics of the layoff survivors in the initial study. Appendix B reports on the human resource interviews.)

The quotations that follow are excerpted from the interview transcripts. They will provide an appreciation of the depth and seriousness of layoff survivor sickness. It is the rare reader who, if employed, will not hear echoes of familiar themes from his own organization.

Survivors' feelings and concerns are separated into fifteen categories: job insecurity; unfairness; depression, stress, and fatigue; reduced risk taking and motivation; distrust and betrayal; optimism; continuing commitment; lack of reciprocal commitment; wanting it to be over; dissatisfaction with planning and communication; anger over the layoff process; lack of strategic direction; lack of management credibility; short-term profit orientation; sense of permanent change.

JOB INSECURITY

Job insecurity was an interview theme that cuts across all levels and was discussed in all groups.

"I go home and I wonder at night am I going to be here tomorrow, the next day, or three days from now?" (manager).

"I find it frightening. At my age, I would really hate to

go out and walk the sidewalks. I wouldn't even know which sidewalk to start on. I think it's very frightening" (clerical employee).

"I've come up through the ranks. I started in assembly. I don't have a college degree, and now I'm doing work [for which] other companies hire those people with master's degrees. If I was tapped on the shoulder tomorrow, and they said, 'Well, find a job,' I don't know where I would find one. If I went outside, I probably wouldn't know what to do. I would be lost. That scares me" (professional/technical employee).

UNFAIRNESS

Like job security, unfairness was a theme that came up in all groups. There were two dimensions to the discussions: a sense that top executives and people from other parts of the organization were not doing their share, and perceptions that the choice of who stayed and who left was unfair.

"I think there are too many instances where they took the wrong people. The ones that have kept their jobs are short termers and haven't contributed in the short time they've been here. Then they've taken senior people because they're paid more. They've made a conscious decision to cut these out and keep people whom I don't consider contribute at all" (field employee).

"They're padding their pockets. In the good times the bonuses and everything go to the top executives, and during the bad times the workers get cut out. The company hasn't shown me that they care as much about me" (professional/technical employee).

"I personally feel like I've seen a lot of good people lose their jobs because somebody screwed up down at headquarters" (professional/technical employee).

"I asked my manager how they decide, because I was curious after the layoffs were happening. He said, basically, they go by your performance overall. That's what he told me.

To me it is just like favoritism. . . . If they like you, they'll keep you; if they don't, they won't" (clerical employee).

"Sometimes we hear in the news or in the business reports [about] executive levels and the gold parachutes. It's something that can cause resentment because you feel that these guys have enough connections or networking that if the plug is pulled on them, they're going to land on their feet elsewhere" (administrative employee).

"The criteria are very political. . . . They just laid a guy off who did a super job, and he had been there about eighteen years. He was very, very upset because he had no idea; he worked so hard. And the reason he was upset was because there was another guy at the same level that he felt was doing such a terrible job, and they don't do anything about it" (administrative employee).

DEPRESSION, STRESS, AND FATIGUE

The themes of depression, stress, and fatigue occurred in all discussion groups, and as the first two quotations show, those in leadership roles shared these feelings.

"But I did walk through, talked with a lot of people. . . . My biggest personal reaction to a lot of what went on was the feeling of depression as I would talk to people" (executive).

"You see a lot of good people being let go and that's very demoralizing, to know that an excellent person is being let go. It affects your credibility with your company, and it also affects your productivity" (manager).

"I walk around with a knot in my stomach. Honestly, two weeks ago I told my boss I'd either take a week off or I'd quit. I had to get away from the job, away from the paper, away from the dispatchers, away from the problems, the customers" (field employee).

REDUCED RISK TAKING
AND MOTIVATION

Employees at all levels saw a direct relationship between the layoffs and reduced risk taking among the survivors.

"Some of the folks I have talked to in the last couple of months have specifically said it's the ones most outspoken that get hit. [We] had sales representatives who had exceeded quota for several years in a row, and then suddenly they're work force reduced. They were the pushy ones saying, 'I need more product, I need this, I need that,' and the perception was that we've lost the risk takers. We lost the people who are willing to speak up" (executive).

"The most dangerous [result] is refusing to take any risks at all. Keeping your head down. You see that from the executive level all the way down to that programmer whom you're asking to reassign to something. They're looking to see if [the reassignment is] at all dead ended. If it is, they don't want it. The same thing is true of executives" (executive).

"Why should I take a new position within this corporation [with] the risks of that project failing or not being funded next year so that I'm exposed? Why should I take that risk?" (professional/technical employee).

"I don't go that extra step anymore, whereas I [used to take on more, on] my own initiative. Because when I would go that extra, I felt I owed the company that. [Now] I don't necessarily feel like I owe the company that" (field employee).

"I feel there are some people in our department who are afraid to speak up on their feelings about the way things are being run or the way their job is being handled — in the sense that [they think], 'If I see something that goes against the grain, or if I say something about my dissatisfaction here, perhaps the next time our department is looked at as to who should be let go, it will be me, because I am the one who has expressed some dissatisfaction in the way that things are being handled.' I think there's a real fear of that" (administrative employee).

"I think we feel kind of intimidated about speaking up to our management. When it comes time to lay off, they'll think, 'Well, that loudmouth — we don't need her around here.' So I find myself holding back, not saying things I should be able to say and stating my opinion" (clerical employee).

DISTRUST AND BETRAYAL

Feelings of distrust and betrayal emerged as themes in the field, headquarters, and professional/technical groups.

"My attitude is affected by what's gone on in the company, and I'm not so positive when I go out there and work. [I think] 'That's not my problem,' where before my attitude was a lot different. I don't care whether the company, and I say *the company*, can support that customer in the middle of the night. It shouldn't be my problem; it's their problem. Let them find somebody else. I'm not going to go out there. That's the attitude I had to take a couple times because I don't care anymore" (field employee).

"I've lost trust in the company. I've been with them for eleven years, and I have no idea whether or not to trust them anymore because of what you hear positive [from them] about the company. The next day you come in to work and it's 180 people out. You can't believe what they say. My key word is that I've lost trust" (field employee).

OPTIMISM

Some managers and executives expressed a sense of optimism. It was their opinion that necessary tough actions had been taken and that the organization was on a painful but clear road toward recovery. These feelings of optimism were unique to the executive and managerial population.

"I think I feel that, more than ever, I know where the

company is going — especially in the decentralized mode that we're in in our division. We know where we are, and we know what we've got to do in order to survive. It's been pretty well laid out to me and to the people who work for me. I feel good about it. I think that the company is doing things now that it had to do ten years ago, and it's got another five years to go before it's going to get there, and it's going to be bloody. But I feel good about it because the alternative is to get the hell out. If [we] don't do those things, . . . we ain't going to be around" (executive).

"When you look at the beginning of it, we were all in a total survival mode. We had to make changes in the company and downscale the way we were doing things in order to survive. And that's good — the overall change of downscaling the entire staff has been good for the company. There's no question about that" (manager).

"I hear a lot of good vibes about the cooperation of those survivors, or pseudo-survivors, that a meaner, leaner corporation we're going to be, and I'm proud to work for it (manager).

CONTINUING COMMITMENT

Despite the uncertainty, and with layoffs going on around them, some employees expressed a continuing sense of commitment to the organization.

"It's difficult when people are being laid off all around you, but I still feel committed to the company. I get concerned about overmanaging the company on a quarterly basis, but I recognize the need for profitability. I still feel committed to the company" (manager).

"In the last six months, I've turned down two good offers. People say, 'Why? Are you crazy?' And maybe I am, but I still have a commitment to this company. I want to see them succeed. I don't want to bail out and say, 'No, we couldn't get the job done.' That's the way I am. I believe that I should follow a job through, but I still feel insecure in my job, and tomorrow I may not have one, no matter of the fact that I did make that commitment to this company" (field employee).

"I just like doing my job. I look at the organization, and I see a company with a hell of a lot of potential. I mean the products, the services, and the like. I don't want to get laid off, and I don't really want to quit. I don't want to go to some other company because it's not going to be much better anyplace else" (field employee).

LACK OF RECIPROCAL COMMITMENT

Although some employees expressed a continuing commitment to the organization, no one felt the organization had a reciprocal ongoing commitment to him or her. Some were angry and bitter about the abrupt change.

"There seems to be an absolute fundamental change in the company as far as its attitude toward people. People are viewed as commodities. The first reaction to problems is to reduce head count. That fundamental attitude seems to have changed the company. [The change] seems to be permanent" (executive).

"I've talked to people, . . . senior executives [who have] been around twenty, twenty-five years, who have been given two minutes total to see their personnel guy. So what's come out of all that is people just wonder where they stand. The biggest problem, I think, that we have as a company in going forward is, in fact, being able to demonstrate by the behavior of executives and each manager in dealing with their people, that they really give a damn about people as individuals, and [give] some dignity and respect to the people" (executive).

"I think that it is a cultural change that's going on in the industry. I think a lot of people have the feeling that if they went to work for a company, enjoyed the company, and gave the company a day's work for a day's pay, they could stay there until the day they retire. There's not that guarantee anymore. It's been a real wake-up to the American public" (manager).

"They owe me a little bit more than just saying . . . , 'You ought to be grateful that you have a job.' They ought to be grateful that I put eleven years into this company and I've done what I consider to be a good job. I never had a poor performance review" (field employee).

WANTING IT TO BE OVER

There was a widespread desire to get on with the downsizing, to get it over. Employees felt fatigued and drained by the continuing reductions. Some felt misled by what they perceived as unfilled promises that the layoffs would end.

"When you get wave after wave and the statement, 'Just around the corner, just around the corner, we're almost there, things are looking up, things are looking up,' wave after wave after wave, it just emotionally drains you" (executive).

"This thing is dragging out too long and that's what the problem is. We're hearing it from this one, we're hearing it from that one, we're hearing it over there. If everything was done all at one time, at least within a three- or four-month period, but here we're dragging it out six, eight, ten, twelve, fourteen months!" (manager).

"We are essentially over, . . . and all that time there has been low productivity from everybody. I feel that even trying to motivate your people and keep up to speed and do additional work is a very difficult task" (manager).

"I guess it seems like it's never ending. If there had been a large work force reduction in the beginning of the year, or at a particular time, and you say, 'That's it, that's what we're going to do. Now we can go off and do our business,' I think that would be easier for the employees to accept. Our group has been hit two or three times since October. It feels like they came back and said, 'Oops, we need some more money.

Let's take some more,' and then, 'Oops, let's take more.' I don't know when they are going to stop. I don't see the end. There's no light at the end of the tunnel that you can say, 'If I can just make it until here, then I'll be okay'" (professional/technical employee).

DISSATISFACTION WITH PLANNING AND COMMUNICATION

The planning, administration, and communication of layoffs was a topic of widespread discussion. Of particular concern among many was the need for longer notice and a more open flow of information:

"We could have given them a little bit more warning, been up front with them and told them, 'Hey, the end of the year you're going to have to go,' in time for them to go out and find a job. We didn't do that. That made it even a little more strenuous on me. There's a lot of distrust right now. That's going to be tough to overcome" (manager).

"All of a sudden somebody hands you a slip of paper, they have you into personnel, in with your boss, and say, 'We don't need you anymore.' That's rough" (manager).

"Everybody knew there was going to be a layoff, and a janitor comes in on Friday night, brings up thirty boxes, sets them by the elevator. Now, those people went home, and they knew . . . they counted the boxes . . . they knew thirty people were going to go. And nobody knew until Monday morning who the thirty of them were. . . . That's bad news! Nobody slept out of the whole group over the weekend because everybody thought it was going to be [him or her]. Just a little bit of coordination could have prevented something like that" (professional/technical employee).

"If cutbacks are needed, planning how you are going to do a total cutback would be better than doing it in little steps and see where you are and then do a little more" (technical/professional employee).

"If they don't know how to plan for the types of cuts that they put in last year, we've got some real bad problems at the top" (field employee).

"Who is making that decision? Where is it really coming from? How did they decide on this person?" (field employee).

"I think a lot of that came through communication problems. If they would at least let us know in advance what was going on, but they keep saying, 'We're doing fine, we're doing fine,' and then all of a sudden people are gone" (field employee).

"So why aren't they letting us know ahead of time that this is what we're planning and be honest; as everybody's saying, be honest with us and let us deal with it" (field employee).

"Invariably, when you ask them, 'Are there going to be more layoffs?' you're told, 'We don't foresee any, there probably will be some, we don't know.' So it's a real secretive type thing" (production employee).

ANGER OVER THE LAYOFF PROCESS

The groups had widespread anger and concern over how layoff victims were treated. The concern was both for the feelings and dignity of those who left and for what the process said about the organization's values.

"You can say all the right things in that private meeting between you, personnel, and the employee, and handle the situation. Then you are forced to walk them out to their desk, gather up their personal effects in full public view. Employee after employee, going through a whole bunch of them. It's demoralizing for the employee, for the management, for personnel, for the people that are sitting out there on the line; it's just archaic, terrible" (executive).

"Some of the people are ushered out of here coldly, like it's all over and you can't even say goodbye to your friends.

They come in here and clean off their desks at night. All of a sudden, the desk is clear; it's gone. They've disappeared. They've vanished into the woodwork" (professional/technical employee).

"They walk them out the door, which I think is a bad thing. It's a humiliating thing, you shouldn't have to do that. That's one thing they've got to quit. Don't humiliate your employees when you lay them off. It's your fault you hired too many. Don't do that. That's the number one thing they've got to do is quit that damn thing" (professional/technical employee).

"My boss tells me, 'You will do the process. Make the cut. Don't tell me that you can't cut expenses, God damn it, go do it.' But how do I translate that back to the guy who's about to get cut?" (executive).

"It goes to the long-term image that we had of being people centered. I see a lot of people being eliminated where the files don't support the action. And then the organization looks and says, 'Holy cow! We thought this guy was a good guy!' and he doesn't have a job—what's it say about us?" (executive).

LACK OF STRATEGIC DIRECTION

The following quotations illustrate deeply felt concerns, expressed primarily by executives and managers, over the perceived lack of strategic direction and the gap between the strategy planners and the implementers:

"We focus really well on what we're going to do tomorrow, and we're going to try and make it through this year, and we're going to have a profitable year, and the bankers are going to be happy, and Wall Street is going to be happy. But where are we going? What is the direction? I understand the total quality processes and all of that. What I don't understand is what the future is. I don't understand how many more business segments are going to be pulled off because we had this problem. What does that leave us, and what do we have left of the company? So, I think it's more openness, honesty, and real communication on those issues that would

make me personally feel better about where we're going"
(executive).

"We've got short-term cash problems, sure, but we have
a strategy, and by God, if the people down there would just
implement it, we would be okay. That worries the hell out
of me more than anything else" (executive).

LACK OF MANAGEMENT
CREDIBILITY

All groups blamed others, usually a generic "management,"
and felt that what these others said had limited credibility.

"Thursday and Friday, knowing it was coming to this,
I went out and visited all my people, especially at remote sites,
and had a chat with them in groups about this, and just tried
to get a feel for what their morale was—where they felt the
company was right now—and the standard flavor I got out
of everybody was, 'I don't believe what I hear from the corporation'" (manager).

"I think we could say that we do not have confidence
in our upper management" (professional/technical employee).

"They keep saying we're going back to the core business,
but I don't see it. . . . I see absolutely no evidence that indicates that's taking place" (field employee).

"[There are] numerous morale builders. . . . They say
we're going to do this and do this, and then two months later,
somehow, miraculously it's dropped. Nobody's heard of it. . . .
They never follow through with anything as far as you can
see" (field employee).

SHORT-TERM
PROFIT ORIENTATION

"They," the generic management, were perceived by some
as fixated on short-term profits and as willing to pay for them
with work force reductions.

"You've got to understand the only indicator of this whole damn thing is the second quarter profits. They don't know what the business is going to do; the only thing they can do is try to keep a status quo until they look at the second and third quarter profits" (manager).

"I know all they want to do right now is turn a profit, and they'll get as many people as they need to do that. That's short term. They're not looking long term anymore" (field employee).

"I say if we don't make a profit at the end of the first quarter, there's going to be more people that are going to be cut, and they'll just keep cutting and cutting until they make a profit" (field employee).

SENSE OF PERMANENT CHANGE

There was a widespread sense of permanent and sudden change, and this sense resulted in stress, resignation, and fear:

"I've gone through a pretty significant change over the last ten months. Last March, I stood before my group and told them that we were sitting with twenty-six people, and that by the end of the year, we would be at no more than fifteen. That was probably the toughest thing I've had to do since I've been with the company. I've been here over twenty-one years. There is a lot of distrust now. It's like all the work I've done and all the work they did in the past is for nothing" (manager).

"The whole organization is 50 percent of what it was. One of the more stressful things is the fact that a lot of full-time employees who have put an awful lot of life into the company have been going by the boards. That's a lot different than the environment in the past" (manager).

"For the first time, I'm scared, really scared. In my case, it's my whole livelihood. I'm the sole supporter in the family, and it's scary to think about what happens to my kids if I lose my job. I didn't worry about that before, but I sure as hell do now" (production worker).

"I feel generally upset with the whole situation. When I come to work I feel tired, even though I don't have much to do. I've never felt that way before and it isn't fear. I don't give a damn if I get laid off. I'm just tired. That's real news for me" (administrative employee).

"I don't feel good anymore about my decision to come to work here. I made that decision twenty-five years ago, and up until last year, I felt good about it. Not anymore. I don't tell my kids to come and work for this company" (professional/technical employee).

"No one is happy anymore. I think a lot of people are under stress, and it just tends to balloon out and everybody is absorbed by it. You don't have anybody coming in in the morning going, 'God, it's a great day'" (clerical employee).

UNEXPECTED FINDINGS

Most of the study findings were consistent with expectations. According to data from other survivor situations and previous research on layoff survivors (such as Brockner and others, 1986), intense fear, anger, insecurity, depression, and guilt seem to be the core survivor feelings. The perceptions of the layoff survivors in this study were consistent with many of these core feelings. There were, however, some unexpected results.

Few Expressions of Survivor Guilt

Guilt was not identified as a major theme. It was only a minor theme within three of the ten groups. Since other researchers believe that feelings of guilt are central to survivorship (Chapter Three), the absence of these feelings in this study is notable. One explanation could be that guilt is a difficult human emotion for an individual to own and disclose in a group situation. The general concern over management competence, lack of information, and feelings of betrayal may be an external projection of internal guilt feelings. Likewise, the extensive reports of fear, depression, and stress could be an acting out of deeper survivor guilt. Such diagnoses, however, are speculative, and their proof would require individual analysis. Even with such analysis, clear boundaries would be difficult to establish since guilt is an abstract emotion and difficult to distinguish only through symptoms.

Expressions of Optimism

Although they also had feelings of uncertainty, stress, and reduced motivation, some managers and executives expressed feelings of optimism, perceptions that a tough but needed job had been done and that the organization was back on track toward profitability. These perceptions occurred exclusively in the three groups made up of managers and executives.

Since managers and executives were often involved in layoff decisions and administration, they had more control or advance knowledge than other survivors. Their optimism may therefore have been related to participation in the process. By focusing on projected organizational outcomes, managers and executives may also have escaped dealing with their personal feelings.

The feelings and perceptions reported by managers and executives are complex and often contradictory. The same executives who expressed feelings of optimism also expressed strong feelings of depression and reduced risk taking.

Emergence of a Layoff-Survivor Blaming Phenomenon

All groups blamed others. In some cases, they blamed a generic "management," or they blamed the next level up. Top executives blamed other executives or the company president. These feelings were intense across all groups. Dissatisfaction with company direction, management credibility, and long-term strategy were particularly strong among executives, professionals, and managers. This was all the more interesting because these people were responsible for these very functions.

The survivor blaming phenomenon may be a form of projection that serves as a defense mechanism, so that the individual can avoid confronting his or her individual survivor guilt. Certainly, such survivor guilt is discussed throughout the survivor literature, and projection of one's own undesirable traits onto others is a widely recognized ego-defense mechanism.

Thirst for Information

Better, clearer, and more consistent information during layoffs was a survivor's key recommendation. Partially this seemed a reaction to their widespread fear and uncertainty. In addition, executives, managers, and technical professionals said they needed a clearer understanding of the organization's strategy and plans. In a number of cases, survivors perceived a lack of adequate plans, and these survivors' recommendations for improved communication may translate into recommendations for better and more effective planning and goal setting. In a sense, the expressed need for better communication was a form of survivor distrust. Many of the layoff survivors seemed not to trust that management actually had a plan for the survival of the business. The lack of trust that someone in the organization had a plan to pull the organization out of its problems may have helped to produce such survivor feelings as fear, uncertainty, anger, or depression. Or the lack of trust may have arisen from those feelings. Either pattern illustrates the interaction and interdependence of survivor feelings and perceptions.

Sense of Change

Survivors in all groups indicated that the layoffs had triggered changes in their relationship to the organization. Whether they were discussing job security, feelings of betrayal, commitment, or coping strategies, the layoff survivors felt a strong sense of change, and these changes were perceived as permanent and wide-ranging.

LEARNINGS AND IMPLICATIONS

In this chapter I intended the reader to feel the anger, fear, and anxiety of layoff survivors, to be flooded with the depth and intensity of survivor feelings. The organization I studied is not unusual. These survivors are mirrors of other layoff survivors, and most readers will find some themes that are all too familiar for themselves and their organizations. A large number of organizations seem to be populated by people who share these symptoms. The organization studied here is, in fact, in better shape than many since its management recognizes the seriousness of the problem. There are methodological issues (sample bias, group dynamics, and content analysis error) that affect the results of this type of study, and care must be taken in generalizing. Nonethless, learning the true extent of layoff survivors' hurt is important for anyone attempting self- or organizational transformation and empowerment.

Time marched on. The economy continued to decline. The organization struggled for survival. Thanks to a cooperative management, I revisited it five years later. What had happened? The story continues in Chapter Five.

5

Time Does Not Heal
All Wounds:
The Effects of Long-Term
Survivor Sickness

"Our group has been hit two or three times
since October. It feels like they came back
and said, 'Oops, we need some more money.
Let's take some more,' and then, 'Oops, let's
take more.' I don't know when they are going
to stop. I don't see the end. There's no light
at the end of the tunnel that you can say, 'If
I can just take it until here, then I'll be okay.'"

Time, it would appear, does not
heal all wounds. In order to assess the impact of time on layoff
survivor symptoms, a second study took place at the same
organization, five years after the initial effort. The methodology was similar to that of the initial study: group interviews,
using the same standard set of questions, were recorded, tran-
scribed, and analyzed for the major themes. The second
study's scope was more limited (three as opposed to ten groups),
and the content analysis was less rigorous (interviewers and
coders were not separate people.) Nonetheless, this is one of
the few attempts to assess the continuity of layoff survivor

symptoms over time, and the results are of interest to any individual or organization attempting to escape the debilitating effects of layoff survivor sickness.

There were a group of twelve production workers (skilled nonexempt and exempt production engineers) from a manufacturing operation, a group of fourteen engineers and professional/technical employees from a design and development operation, and a group of ten administrative staff from corporate headquarters. For logistical and administrative reasons, managers and executives were not included in this study. Also, unlike the first groups, these groups included only long-term employees (the groups were voluntary, but no one was accepted with less than six years' experience). In reality, the groups attracted very long-term employees; the median length of service was sixteen years. Two of the three groups were in parts of the organization represented in the original sample; owing to organizational changes, the third group, professional/technical employees, represented a blend of three organizational areas, two of which were in the original sample. To protect confidentiality in the first study, no names had been recorded. However, the participants in the second study were asked if any of them had participated in the earlier study, and no one indicated she or he had participated then. Therefore, I assumed that none of the participants in the second study had been in the first study. In the intervening years, the organization had gone through a series of major downsizings and layoffs continued unabated.

What is especially important about the groups in the second study is that the employees grew up under the full flowering of the old employment contract; survived a continuing series of organizational consolidations, spin-offs, and layoffs; and were now attempting to cope with the reality of the new employment contract. They had one foot in the old, another in the new, their heart was on the border between the old and the new, and their spirit was infected with layoff survivor sickness. The reader will come closer to feeling the concerns of these survivors by once again reviewing the raw data rather than abstracts of results.

STRESS, FATIGUE, EXTRA WORKLOAD, DECREASED MOTIVATION, SADNESS, AND DEPRESSION

The symptoms of stress, fatigue, decreased motivation, sadness, and depression, combined with an extra workload, persisted over the five-year time frame. The sense of resignation, fatigue, and depression seemed heavier and more pronounced.

"I didn't realize that I was probably suffering from some form of depression, but it was going on, and on, and on. I mean day after day after day, feeling the same way" (administrative employee).

"Everything is negative, and when you do good things it's not recognized; whether it's the media, whether it's your manager, everything is always, in my opinion, on the down. So, when you come to work, you are on the down" (professional/technical employee).

"It's much worse just by accumulation. It's gone on for so long" (professional/technical employee).

"I kind of look back to when the layoffs first started, back in the mid-eighties, and I felt very devastated by it. I felt very sad for these people, and, personally, as it started to continue on, I felt like the people who were left kind of got callous. Now it's gotten so commonplace that I think sometimes we hardly say goodbye" (administrative employee).

INSECURITY, ANXIETY, AND FEAR

The symptoms of insecurity, anxiety, and fear also continued. There was an attempt that was not always successful to understand and accommodate a state of permanent job insecurity.

"One thing none of us have come up with is a model of how to behave in a situation like this. We grew up with [the] model that our parents worked hard and they didn't have as much as we do, but it seemed, in the eyes of a child, [to have] more safety in it. Now we're adults; we're fifty years old, and we don't have an example in our life to follow as to what to do when you're fifty and the rug is totally pulled out from under you. It's a little more difficult at a mature stage to go back and act like a teenager and say, 'Oh boy, the whole world is great!' I think it is hard for us to do that because people are watching us: our spouses, our children, our parents, our sisters, our brothers. There is a sense that you have done something wrong if you get laid off. I don't think anyone escapes that. Even if, in their rational minds, they say, 'I was good, it just happened to be the job I was in.' There's something down deep that says, 'You weren't good enough, there's something wrong, you pissed somebody off, you didn't play the game'" (administrative employee).

"The only way you provide security for yourself is by making sure that your work experience is as up-to-date as possible so that if tomorrow happens, you are able to go out and get another job, because you have the skills people want. That's the only way you have security. You aren't going to get it from the company. It will never be that way again" (professional/technical employee).

"Five years ago, you felt more secure. You had a future with the company. At the present time, you don't know whether you are going to be sold out, you are going to be downsized. That's a big difference" (professional/technical employee).

"Decisions on . . . should I buy a car, should I put a new roof on the house, these are things that have been on hold. I don't see an end in sight. My boss says, 'I don't know what the plan is, and I'm not going to ask'" (administrative employee).

LOYALTY TO JOB (NOT COMPANY), NONRECIPROCAL LOYALTY, AND SELF-RELIANCE

There seemed to be a much stronger feeling among the second round of layoff survivors that the organization was not in the business of "looking out for its employees," and that their loyalty was to themselves and to their unit, not to the overall organization.

"I am committed to my customers. I am committed to the people who use my services, and it doesn't matter where I work, it's the people that I work with that I really enjoy, and I really want to do a good job for them" (administrative employee).

"Well, if it goes, I've had a wonderful time. They've paid for my daughter's education, and the food in my mouth, and lots of things over the years. I guess what they're talking about now is, they can't promise us life security forever. No company can" (administrative employee).

"At one time, we kind of felt the company was responsible for your job security and that they would look after you, but I think we all know today that has shifted" (professional/technical employee).

"I think it's changed dramatically. For myself it has. And I think we see that from the company's side too. Many meetings that we've had, we've been told, 'You're responsible for your future.' It's not like it used to be" (administrative employee).

"The distinction for me that it isn't necessarily a commitment to the company, it's a commitment to the kind of work that I do. So it's a commitment to my own self, and it's a commitment to my department, too. But not necessarily a commitment to the company" (administrative employee).

SENSE OF UNFAIRNESS AND ANGER OVER TOP MANAGEMENT PAY AND SEVERANCE

These survivors had much more anger than the earlier survivors over the perceived unfairness of top management severance and bonus payments.

"There was such a wave of anger that people felt about

that. It was shameful to be part of the organization, that they would do that!" (administrative employee).

"We took away from employees, we took away from retirees, we took away from everybody. Where did it go? Right to those people that walked out the door with the million-dollar parachutes. It was so shameful! Even now, after all these years, I realize everybody has the same anger about it" (administrative employee).

"My message to top management is that you should spend as much time as you use trying to figure out how your gold parachute can do good for you, take that same energy and start making the company work. It's absolutely unacceptable for people to walk away with that kind of money in a downsized environment. Absolutely unacceptable! You have no credibility at all" (professional/technical employee).

"I never felt so angry in my life. When I had gone out and stood up to all kinds of people who said, 'Oh yes, you work for that great company. Nobody can be that good.' I defended them, and then the company still wants the same kind of commitment out of me! My time, my hours, my life! No, I'm too old for that!" (administrative employee).

RESIGNATION AND NUMBNESS

There appeared to be an increase in the sense of resignation and numbness. One survivor seemed embarrassed to tell outsiders where she worked.

"I think that when it first started I felt confident that things would get better. I don't feel that way anymore. I don't think my feelings about the losses have changed. I feel, I think, just as horrible as the day when one person loses their job as I did when ten thousand did, but what made me feel better then was I felt we were going to turn a corner. Things were going to get better. I don't think that I'm a pessimist at all, but I don't see any evidence that we're turning any corner" (administrative employee).

"Twenty-five years ago there was a real sense of group and a sense of two-way loyalty that was very strong. I see none of that anymore. There's no sense of continuity. I see a lot of people that seem to spend as much emotional energy in preparing for possibly losing their job [and positioning] themselves to get another job, should that actually happen, as they do in actually doing their job" (professional/technical employee).

"On the floor there are a lot of guys who would just as soon get it over with, get it done. They are just tired of going through it every three months. They feel unemployed. Something's got to give; it's just not right" (production employee).

"Sometimes I almost feel like an idiot just for staying here this long. When people ask me where I work, I feel like an idiot when I tell them" (production employee).

"It's always downsizing. We hear that so much, you almost become numb. All of us think, 'Well, who's next?' It's always something. It never seems to just settle down and let us work for a little while. It's constant pressure. It's not a happy environment to be in for me" (professional/technical employee).

LACK OF MANAGEMENT COMMUNICATION

Although five years had passed, the thirst for information and the survivor blaming phenomenon continued to be important.

"People are interested in having a company make money because that's how we get paid, but a lot of management's concept of communication is to put out a financial report. There's a lot more to it than that" (professional/technical employee).

"We call them sunshine meetings because it comes across like everything is wonderful, and two weeks later there's another layoff" (production employee).

"I think [lack of communication is] a true dynamic with all downsizing. [But] some management withholds information for purposes of power, security. It's threatening for them to let go of too much information" (administrative employee).

"The truth gets lost. I go to communication meetings with the higher-level managers, and the numbers they're putting up on the charts are absolutely impossible when you are out on the floor and you know what's going on" (production employee).

HELPFUL AND COMMUNICATIVE MANAGERS

Not all survivors blamed all managers. Some saw certain managers as accessible and as facilitators of communication. One production employee saw the issue as middle manager involvement:

"My immediate manager, I can talk to him about what's going on real comfortably, and he's more worried about his job than I am with mine. He's gone through six location changes, so he knows what it's all about. He's pretty open, pretty honest. He's even told me to polish up my résumé, that it wouldn't hurt to send it around because things aren't looking good" (production employee).

"To the defense of management, they're trying to find their spot too. They don't know where they belong either. They don't know what's going on with them the next time either" (administrative employee).

"In our department, I see that top management is trying very hard and is trying to squeeze out the management that isn't going to make this company go forward by meeting with employee groups and empowering them, by bypassing all these other layers. But I think that we might be looking for some of what we had in the past, and we're not going to have that, and I do believe that top management is communicating, but I think they need to just come out a little bit stronger" (administrative employee).

"I will say in defense of these men that they are working their fannies off right now" (administrative employee).

"I would like to say about top management that I think they have the right spirit. They talk about empowering the people, letting the people have more authority to make changes and stuff like that, but unless they get middle management motivated to get involved in some of the changes that the employees are trying to make, it's not going to happen" (production employee).

HONEST COMMUNICATION

All groups were very clear on their need for direct, open communication. This concern for straight talk was not as pronounced in the initial study.

"Treat us like adults. Treat us like we can handle the real information" (administrative employee).

"I think it is time to show us that we are really going to do something besides liquidate" (administrative employee).

"You should never suppress any information because it can come back to haunt you. Be very honest, and I think most people will accept things if you are honest with them. I think you can get in trouble when you skirt around the issues and act like nothing's going on" (professional/technical employee).

"[They should] be stronger in their decisions . . . instead of riding the fence. Say yes or no" (professional/technical employee).

"All of us have to make decisions every day, but just be honest. I think that's the answer" (professional/technical employee).

"I guess I would say, 'If nothing else, just please be honest with us'" (production employee).

"Tell us something that sounds like it's coming from someone's heart and not from their ledger" (administrative employee).

SHORT-TERM PLANS AND STRATEGY

Survivors in the professional/technical group, which had experienced the most mergers and organizational change, expressed dissatisfaction with short-term planning. However, the concern was more limited and focused than in the initial study.

"It's quarter-by-quarter management, and that really hurts. If you are in a declining environment and you manage strictly quarter by quarter, you will never grow" (professional/technical employee).

"The number one objective for the last several years has been quarterly profit. . . . In order to make that quarterly profit, we've had indirect people have to take time off without pay, whatever it takes to make that quarterly profit. And if that's all you're looking at, one quarter ahead—I mean, we have these long-range strategic plans, but they seem kind of pie-in-the-sky because we are always focusing quarter by quarter. There's no real long-range philosophy. You don't see that practiced" (professional/technical employee).

"Last July when they came through, so-and-so sat down and looked at the numbers, management came in with some numbers, and we were so many million short, and they said, 'Go back and come up with some new numbers.' We [had] just cut down thirty-one people. 'Try fifteen or twenty more in September—do it!' And that gets out to us folks, and we say, 'Why are they doing that?' It just doesn't make sense" (professional/technical employee).

"They really think that manpower planning and skills can be turned on and off like a faucet as opposed to a smooth flowing, blending arrangement" (professional/technical employee).

LAYOFF PROCESS PROBLEMS

Survivors in the second study told the same kinds of horror stories concerning the way layoffs were handled as the earlier survivors. However, they seemed clear on the difference between "good" and "bad" process.

"I think that [layoffs] are handled very poorly. I worked with a guy for twenty-two years. We knew there was going to be a layoff in our department, but nobody was told ahead of time who it was going to be. When the day arrived, it was minutes before quitting time, and the boss came down and told him, 'You're it.' He had to pack his tools, clean out. It was a big shock. I don't think it was a very fair way of treating someone who has worked for a company for twenty-two years" (production employee).

"I see that a lot. The people who actually have the person-to-person contact with the person who is being laid off aren't the ones who made the decision. They often didn't have any input into which of their people would go. There is something wrong with that process" (professional/technical employee).

"I think it's a shotgun approach to how you maintain numbers and how to get rid of people legally without getting taken to court" (professional/technical employee).

"I don't think any of us can get hold of any data that says, 'This is the process of how to treat a person humanely when you lay them off.' There are terrible managers, and there are good ones. I think [among] individual managers some do a good job and some do a bad job" (professional/technical employee).

"I'm often in a position to be talking to people very shortly after they have been given notice, and I can get very angry seeing the difference between when it's done well and when people have been left with so many unanswered questions" (administrative employee).

"You really see a difference in the process, if they are treated well than if they are not" (administrative employee).

"Compassion makes a huge difference. In some cases, you can tell there wasn't any in existence" (administrative employee).

RESENTMENT OVER BEING
MADE TO FEEL GUILTY

The headquarters administrative group expressed two themes that did not come out in the earlier study: resentment over being told to be thankful they had a job, and a perception that being positive was countercultural.

"I get angry when I get out on the line and I hear management and [human resources] saying to their employees, 'You're just damned lucky you have a job. Go away and quit complaining'" (headquarters administrative employee).

"[They say], 'Don't complain. You're lucky you have a job.'" (administrative employee).

"It gets difficult to just come in and say, or for managers to say, 'You're lucky you have a job.' It's more difficult for me to even feel that I am one of the lucky ones. I'm still staying here, and I'm going through all of these changes. The other people at least know where they are and, hopefully, know where they are going to go, or at least they are in the process of going somewhere" (administrative employee).

"It's not that . . . I'm feeling cheated because I'm not let go, but I do feel it's very difficult to come in and continue to be positive about being a survivor when there are some people out there saying, 'You're damned lucky you've got a job.'" (administrative employee).

"Are you really lucky, or are they the lucky ones because they've left?" (administrative employee).

"You have to justify it, that you're still here. Even when you walk out of here, you meet somebody and you say where you work, and they say, 'How did you survive?' It just kind of feels that even to the outside world you have to justify yourself, that you're still there—'How do you rate that you still have a job?' Why do I have to justify myself? It wasn't me who stood there and said, 'I want this job.' They kept me for one reason or another. I don't know why, but they probably have their reasons" (administrative employee).

"My positiveness has oftentimes been almost a negative

because everybody's so down. They feel I am insensitive, that I'm naive, that I don't know what's going on around me, which is not the case" (administrative employee).

"I think it can make people feel uncomfortable if you seem to be having a good time in this environment" (administrative employee).

LEARNINGS AND IMPLICATIONS

Layoff survivor symptoms have persevered and evolved over time within the organization. Survivors seem more tired and depressed. They seem to have been ground down by five years of job insecurity and flux. Although they have reduced their reliance on the organization to take care of them and seem resigned to nonreciprocated loyalty, they are still struggling to understand and accommodate permanent job insecurity. They are an angry group, with much of their ire focused on top executive compensation and severance payments. They have little tolerance for false optimism and fuzzy answers. They want straight talk and honest communication. Some employees resented being made to feel guilty over simply surviving and having a job. Others expressed resentment over being made to feel they did not understand the environment because their behavior was positive.

Again, owing to the narrow sample and methodology used, care must be taken with any generalization; however, the data from this study, other survivor studies, my experience, and feedback from a number of colleagues all show that survivor symptoms do not automatically go away on their own. They remain, evolve, and often intensify over time.

Layoff survivor sickness is complicated, and the cure does not lend itself to a one-dimensional prescription. The next chapter introduces a four-level model of intervention for curing this complex disease.

Part Three

Interventions for Healthy Survival

6

A Four-Level Process
for Handling Layoffs
and Their Effects

"I feel generally upset with the whole
situation. When I come to work I feel tired,
even though I don't have much to do. I've
never felt that way before and it isn't fear. I
don't give a damn if I get laid off. I'm just
tired. That's real news for me."

Beneath the sterile and analytical reports of organizational downsizings, mergers, and restructurings lurks something that is decidedly not as antiseptic as the sanitized reports would lead you to believe. Turn over the layoff rock in most organizations and you will find some ugly and toxic creatures. The few of us who have both turned the rock over and written about what we have seen have all seen the same creatures. However, like the blind people exploring the elephant, each of us has had a different view of these phenomena and labeled this view accordingly. It is the "dirty dozen": a combination of scapegoating, decreasing morale, increased conflict, and other "dysfunctional effects" (Cameron, Kim, and Whetten, 1987). It is the acting out of survivor guilt

(Brockner and others, 1986). It is a combination of guilt,
depression, loss of control, increased substance abuse, sleep-
lessness, and tension (Marks, 1991b). It is a form of depression that leads to wasting away (Harvey, 1981). Despite the
varying labels, what is becoming increasingly clear to everyone is the magnitude of damage done by these phenomena.

Layoffs are often seen as a subset of overall downsizing
strategies. However, the symptoms of layoff survivor sickness
are a major barrier to productivity gains. In an extensive best-
practice survey of automotive industry downsizing, Kim Cameron, Sarah Freeman, and April Mishra (1991) found evidence
of survivor guilt. They also found that one characteristic of
firms with the best practices was paying special attention to
survivors, which they implied was successful in alleviating survivor guilt. However, the way most of the downsizings were
implemented had caused quality and productivity to deteri-
orate rather than increase. Consulting companies, long in the
front lines of the downsizing movement, have made similar
reports. A study of over one thousand downsized organizations by the Wyatt Company (1991) indicated that most of
these organizations did not meet their initial goals. Mitchell
and Company (Dorfman, 1991) followed sixteen large restructurings from 1982 to 1988. At the end of this period, the organizations' stock performance trailed that of their competition
by an average of 26 percent. In a survey of 909 managers, Right
Associates (1992) found that 70 percent reported that survivors
felt insecure about their future and had reduced confidence
in their ability to manage their own careers. Seventy-two percent of the managers indicated that the survivors felt the re-
structured organization was not a better place to work.

LAYOFF SURVIVOR
FEELING CLUSTERS
AND COPING STRATEGIES

Whether layoff survivor sickness is perceived as the result of
ineffective downsizings (Cameron, Freeman, and Mishra,

1991) or as a moral issue caused by collusion and a lack of courage (Harvey, 1988), the outcome is the same. Layoffs have drained the work spirit, creativity, and productivity from many of our organizations. The stories of survivors of more traumatic events, my own experience with downsized organizations, and layoff-survivor research all show that layoff survivors experience the following feelings.

Feeling Clusters

Although general "clusters" of feelings are apparent among layoff survivors, the research has not shown any universal hierarchy of causality for these feelings. Of course, every individuals' definition of a particular emotion is slightly different from others' definitions, so these clusters are broad rather than narrow. For example, some survivors saw depression and fatigue as outgrowths of stress, while others described stress as a result of fatigue and depression. Also, the stories of other survivors suggest that a strong theme of guilt might have been expected to emerge in the study presented in Chapters Four and Five. One reason this guilt did not appear may be that guilt is difficult to disclose. However, the survivor blaming phenomenon is seen by some researchers as a projection of guilt feelings. Layoff survivors' extensively reported fear, depression, and stress may likewise be emotions reflecting a deeper survival guilt.

However, the clusters of feelings that follow may be considered a working definition of layoff survivor sickness.

- *Fear, insecurity, and uncertainty.* These feelings cluster together, are among the easier ones to identify, and are found in every layoff survivor situation.

- *Frustration, resentment, and anger.* Layoff survivors are often unable to openly express these emotions within their organization. The suppression of these emotions creates further problems.

- *Sadness, depression, and guilt.* Layoff survivors often mask depression and sadness in order to fit in with a false group bravado or to "hang tough" in the post-layoff period. However, these feelings are usually easier to spot than guilt, which is often suppressed and manifested in other behavior.

■   *Unfairness, betrayal, and distrust.* These feelings are often acted out through coping mechanisms such as blaming others and a seemingly insatiable need for information.

Coping Methods

Layoff survivors cope with their feelings in ways that are neither personally healthy nor organizationally productive.

■   *Reduced risk taking.* Layoff survivors tend to hunker down in the trenches. They report risk-averse behavior, reluctance to take on new products, and fear of finishing existing ones. They are seen as becoming more rigid and conservative.

■   *Lowered productivity.* Layoff survivors are initially consumed with seeking information and understanding their new environment, rather than producing, but the relationship between survivor stress and productivity is complex. Some evidence exists that moderate job insecurity will increase productivity (Brockner, 1992). As time progresses and layoff symptoms solidify, it would appear that survivors lose their work spirit and creativity.

■   *Unquenchable thirst for information.* Layoff survivors soak up and demand information. Questing for information not only from formal channels and newspapers but also from rumors and nonverbal messages from management is a core survivor coping mechanism.

■   *Survivor blaming.* Layoff survivors cope by blaming others, usually those above them, a generic management. Top managers tend to blame the chief executive officer (CEO), each other, or those below them. CEOs I have worked with tend to blame the economy, competition, other executives, the work ethic, or in one case, the labor union.

- *Justification and explanation.* This is a coping method for those "in the know," those involved in layoff administration. I have observed it most in staff managers and executives: lawyers, public relations executives, accountants, and human resource managers. I found it among the human resource professionals in the major organization I studied (see Appendix B). These professionals spent a great deal of time and energy on explaining and justifying the need for layoffs.

- *Denial.* Many organizations exhibit a hierarchical pattern of denial. The higher a person is in the organization, the greater his or her denial. This denial chain must be broken before any meaningful intervention strategy can be implemented.

Persistence of Symptoms over Time

Other survivors' symptoms do not go away on their own and neither do layoff survivors' symptoms. They require an intervention. Not only do these symptoms persist over time but certain of them seem to intensify.

- *Increase in resignation, fatigue, and depression.* In organizations undergoing continuing reductions and change, survivors seem to lose their spark, be flat and tired, and simply go through the motions without hope.

- *Deepening sense of loss of control.* Long-term layoff survivors tend to give the organization control of their work life and, often, their self-esteem. Instead of taking control of their own destiny, they hang on and wait for external events to direct them.

- *Heightened and more focused anger.* Long-term layoff survivors are very angry. Compared to the anger of others, their anger seems sharpened and more personally focused. In the large organization study, this anger was directed at top executive compensation and severance payments. In other organizations, the anger is focused more on individuals and is a clear extension of the survivor blaming phenomenon.

THE FOUR-LEVEL
INTERVENTION MODEL

Layoff survivor sickness is serious. It is complex and does not lend itself to a simple solution. It contains conflicts of values centered on organizational codependency and self-empowerment. To be cured of it, people must let go of the familiar old, and venture into the untested new. Healing layoff survivor sickness is, in the final analysis, an individual effort, requiring great personal courage. Creating organizational systems that will prevent the reoccurrence of this sickness ought to be one of the most fundamental priorities of organizational leaders.

Only compelling interventions can deal with the pathology of layoff survivor sickness. These *interventions* will be powerful acts, attention-grabbing and stimulating forces that compel survivors to choose personal and organizational change.

Four levels of intervention are needed to deal with layoff survivor sickness (Figure 6.1).

1. *Process interventions.* Level 1 interventions deal with the process, the way layoffs take place from the survivors' perspective. These interventions do not provide a cure for survivor sickness, but keep survivors from sinking further into survivor symptoms.

2. *Grieving interventions.* Level 2 interventions help survivors grieve. These interventions deal with repressed feelings and emotions and provide the opportunity for a catharsis that releases the energy that has been invested in emotional repression.

Figure 6.1. Four-Level Intervention Model.

3. *Interventions that break the chain of organizational co-dependency.* Level 3 interventions help survivors recapture from the organization their sense of control and self-esteem.

4. *Systems interventions.* Level 4 interventions create the structural systems and processes that immunize people against survivor sickness.

Although the four-level pyramid is a stage model (Level 1 interventions proceed to Level 2 and so on) and is intended to convey the increasing depth and breadth of each successive intervention, the real world is much more dynamic than any model. Level 1 process interventions sometimes lead directly to Level 4 system changes without going through Levels 2 or 3. Breaking the shackles of organizational codependency (Level 3) often stimulates Level 2 grieving and vice versa. The four-level model is a general conceptual one, not an exact road map. However, the model generally holds true: process interventions are less complex and deep than those that facilitate grieving; interventions to break organizational codependency are yet deeper and broader than the first two; while interventions that change organizational systems from those that reinforce the old paradigm to those that encourage the new are the most difficult of all.

LEARNINGS AND IMPLICATIONS

Mergers, downsizings, and the resultant layoffs are not as neat, tidy, and sterile as accountants and security analysts make them out to be. Those looking under layoff rocks have found both sad and toxic thoughts and feelings. They are not always labeled in the same manner by all rock turners, but under any name they are hazardous to individual and organizational health. In my findings, layoff survivor sickness is not cured by a simple prescription. In the next four chapters, I will describe the four-level intervention model that can reduce layoff survivor sickness.

7

Level One:
Manage the
Layoff Processes

"Compassion makes a huge difference.
In some cases, you can tell there wasn't any
in existence."

Level 1 interventions affect the
layoff processes and their impact on survivors. Although Level
1 interventions occur at the tip of the layoff iceberg, they are
tactically important. They keep survivors from sinking too
deeply into the quagmire of depression and guilt, keeping
these survivors afloat until other, more permanent interventions can be applied to pull them out. Most layoff planners
work out the processes of severance pay, communications se-
quencing, benefits, outplacement services, and often (sadly)
how desks get cleaned out and victims are escorted to the
door, with little or no thought of the impact on those who

stay. Line managers and staff groups commonly spend days obsessing over the most intricate details of notification and implementation, with no consideration of the survivors. However, recent studies (Davy and Tansik, 1986; Brockner, 1992) point out that layoff processes have major effects on survivors too. Survivors' involvement in the decision-making process, their level of attachment to the victims, and their perception as to the fairness and equity of layoffs have all been documented as important process factors that planners should consider.

"CLEAN KILLS" AND THE SURVIVOR HYGIENE FACTOR

Frederick Herzberg (1964) developed a motivational theory that divides motivational factors into those that do motivate (such as satisfaction with the work itself), and those that simply keep employees from becoming *de*motivated (such as pay and working conditions). Herzberg calls the latter "hygiene factors." Level 1 interventions are the layoff equivalent of Herzberg's hygiene factors: they do not cure survivor sickness, but they blunt its symptoms and permit a more rapid recovery. When I explained this concept to a battle-weary manager who was planning yet another round of layoffs, he summed up my elegant theory by saying, "You mean a clean kill is better than a messy one!" Despite the violent language, a survivor symptom in itself, his response contains a hard truth, and it conjured up a vivid image from my youth in Minnesota. I remember a grizzled professional hunter standing on a snow-covered knoll, rifle in hand, thinning out a herd of deer who did not have enough food to survive a tough winter. Doing it right, making a "clean," direct kill, was better than making a mess of it, leaving a wounded animal lurching through the herd. The clean process did not ensure the survival of all the remaining deer, but it did prevent a collective panic.

REDUNDANT COMMUNICATION IS ESSENTIAL

Layoff survivors have an unquenchable thirst for information, before, during, and after reductions. Their need leaps from the pages of data in Chapters Four and Five in this book. It is impossible for managers to overcommunicate during layoffs. Survivors suck up data like desert sand absorbs water. They are information junkies. If they do not get needed information, they go through withdrawal and then guess at what's going on and develop theories based on fragments of information. If you are a layoff planner, it is extremely important for you to respond to this need. Flood the system with information—oral, written, formal, informal, verbal, and nonverbal; up, down, and laterally—over and over again. You cannot communicate enough! Even when you know you are saying the same thing to the same audience in the same way, you need to redouble the effort. I have yet to find an organization that has satisfied layoff survivors' information hunger.

WHAT TO COMMUNICATE

Layoff planners should *communicate everything that is going on.* During layoffs employees are not concerned only with the obvious questions of who is going, when they are going, and how they were chosen. Employees are desperately seeking assurance and striving for control over a frightening environment. They want to know that the cafeteria will be operational, the paychecks will not bounce, the softball league will continue, the dental plan will stay in effect, the Monday morning staff meeting will still take place. You name it, they want to know about it. Written communication is important, but writing memos and flooding the system with paper alone is not enough. A surprising number of employees have difficulty reading, and others simply prefer oral information. But hearing or reading information is not enough for employees either; they want to see it and not just on video. Nonverbal messages are stronger than words. Bosses must be visible. They do not need to exhibit false bravado; they do need to be authentic. Eye contact; touching, if it fits the culture, or handshakes; and empathic body language are the currency of authenticity. Managers should think of how they would behave when they are the authority figure at a funeral or during a time of crisis, confusion, or emotional tension in a small group or family. The bottom has just dropped out from the survivors' world, and they are in dire need of consistency and continuity. Managers and top executives have similar needs. When they become involved in communicating to employees, they will also reassure themselves.

Despite the overwhelming evidence that there is a data feeding frenzy at all levels, it is often difficult for managers to stimulate and maintain the free flow of information. Instead, during layoffs managers often set for themselves what I call *control traps*, barriers that block needed self-insight and authentic communication.

THREE CONTROL TRAPS
THAT BLOCK COMMUNICATION

Free-flowing communication, emotional honesty, and personal authenticity are the basic ingredients of Level 1 interventions. It is, therefore, important to confront and spring the jaws of the control traps that block communication, honesty, and authenticity.

Control Trap 1: Managing Communication
Managers set up this control trap when they artificially manage and monitor the natural, authentic communiction flow. In nearly every organization, there is someone who has a

vested interest in managing information. In normal times, this activity falls to the staff function that handles external public relations and internal employee communication. Usually the strategy is to control the way things are said — or often, not said — so that the organization and especially top management look good, or at least do not look bad. In times of crisis, the strategy is to tighten up these controls. Top managers' announcements are carefully crafted and scripted. Their "spontaneous" comments to employees while "walking around" are often rehearsed. At the very time when organizational leaders need to be most human and accessible to their fellow employees, they become most artificial and controlled.

Earlier I suggested that managers think of how they would behave at a funeral. What effect would it have on surviving family members if the authority figure communicated from clear, conservative scripts, written in advance by lawyers? In organizations facing layoffs, contrived leadership communication does not fool anyone; employees see right through it.

At the very time when authentic and empathetic communication is needed, what is delivered is often controlled and cold. This does not mean that top managers and the staffers who write their scripts are bad people. In fact, they too are survivors, and their attempts to control interpersonal relationships are, at one level, a means of escaping from the authentic sharing of emotions that would help purge their survivor symptoms and force them to give up their denial of these symptoms. Therefore the attempt to control communication is a particularly toxic form of denial, one that separates top management from the rest of the organization and leads to the bunker mentality found in many executive suites at the time of layoffs.

Employees at the opposite end of the organizational hierarchy are not immune to their own version of this control trap. They displace their fear and anxiety through anger at management. They control their own communication by developing ritualistic blaming behavior that speaks of "we" and "they." Much of their communication can be seen as a projection of their anger. This control trap allows them to escape the painful but necessary task of exploring their survivor guilt and depression. The end result of overmanaged communication at the top and ritualized blaming at lower levels is a politicized organization in which all real communication has been shut down at the time when the organization most needs authenticity.

All levels need the courage to go against the grain. For top managers, this is the courage to interact authentically and naturally with their fellow survivors. It often means ignoring, or at least tempering, the advice of lawyers and communication experts. While managers should not say and do things that will result in lawsuits or will hurt people, it is my experience that there is a wide gap, often a chasm, between the kind of communication that will be harmful to the organization or its people and the kind that normally takes place during a crisis situation such as a layoff.

It is genuinely lonely at the top, and top executives become further isolated during downsizings and layoffs. They need someone to talk to. Some hire a consultant not so much for the consultant's management advice as for someone to listen to their sadness over having to terminate their fellow employees and their frustration over being the one fate designated to make the hard decisions. Many of the executives I have worked with have not shared their natural human feelings with anyone inside or outside the organization. At the same time, they have a deep and suppressed need to share these feelings with their fellow survivors because this sharing would also be a way of asking for absolution for executive actions. Employees have a reciprocal need to hear that the top manager is human and authentic and shares their pain. It is a tragic irony when neither need is met because top executives believe that they are expected to manage not only the organization but also the authenticity of their emotions.

Control Trap 2: Managing Emotions

Even at the best of times it is unacceptable to talk about feelings and emotions in most executive suites. The air at the top is dry, analytical, and rational. When people ascend to the top of an organization, they do not leave their feelings and emotions behind, but they do enter a culture in which issues are not seen as warm and messy but as cool and orderly. Shareholders, security analysts, bankers, and years of tradition mold corporate executives' behavior, while secretaries, senior staffers, walled-off offices, and executive garages and lunchrooms serve to protect and seal off the top from the middle.

Does that mean there is no stress at the top? No way! Leading a complex hierarchical organization is a difficult, unpredictable, and enormously stressful job. Moreover, because there is no culturally acceptable external outlet for this stress, it is internalized. Top executives are like ice cubes that have not quite frozen. They are cool and firm on the outside, but tepid and viscous on the inside. Most executive suites are not healthy places to dwell over time! When the guilt and anger generated by survivor sickness are added to this normal stress, executives' initial and often only response is to redouble the effort to manage their emotions.

Organizational leaders are often "helped" in this response by their staffers. Human resource people buffer and filter the executive impact of a fearful and anxious work force. Communication officers write speeches and sanitize official communiqués. Lawyers find Teflon words that hedge and equivocate. As a result of this institutionalized management of emotions, any honest attempt to make a human contact with survivors is stifled.

Employees at the lower end of the organization also manage their emotions. At times they are victims of cultural trickle-down, as they emulate the mushy ice cube culture at the top. Much of the time their own past socialization also encourages a controlled response. It is not easy or culturally acceptable, particularly for males, to talk about their real feelings. It is more acceptable to joke or engage in the kind of projection that leads to blaming others.

The control trap of managing emotions leads to isolation at the top, projection and repression at the bottom, and a mixture of both in the middle. Managers can break out of this trap through Level 2 interventions, which I will discuss later. Briefly, these interventions involve facilitating dialogues about feelings. The focus of the first dialogue is intrapersonal, as the facilitator helps survivors get in touch with their true underlying feelings. The next dialogue is interpersonal, as the facilitator helps survivors to talk to each other.

Control Trap 3: Managing an Unproductive Image

Image management is an artifact of the old employment contract. Wear the right clothes, say the right things, live in the right suburb, join the right club, and you will, if you keep doing these things correctly, rise up in the organization. Individuals often act out unproductive or irrelevant images. The new MBA from a prestigious quantitatively oriented school, who feels able to master any situation through decision matrices and analytical thought, suffers a severe dose of reality when he or she encounters the unpredictable, time-constrained, confusing, and ambiguous realities of organizational life. The prevailing image of management as a controlling, evaluating, analytical function is not productive when the management skills needed for results are empathy, sharing, and authenticity. Leaders who rose up by perpetuating the image of control are armed with the wrong tools to be useful in organizations suffering from layoff survivor sickness. These leaders need a new self-perception, one that emphasizes helping others and honest communication.

The following example shows how strong the image of control can be. In one organization, a low-level executive who had just received word that he had to go attended a regularly scheduled staff meeting where all in attendance knew he had, only that morning, become a layoff victim. This was an "up-or-out" organization, where professionals had a limited time to make partner. If they failed, they had either to leave or to accept the fact that they were plateaued. The norm was macho and tough. It was not safe to get too close to one's peers because they were also competitors. Not one person in that meeting said a thing about what had happened, even though it was obvious that the laid-off executive was hurting. Later, individual attendees expressed their anger and sympathy, but indicated that any public statement of anger or sympathy would not be good for their image.

Breaking Control Traps

Individuals break control traps through insight, coaching, support, and a great deal of personal courage. Top executives are bright people and cognitively recognize the harm of control traps. But it takes coaching, support, and feedback for them to turn their cognition into behavior. It takes courage for them to go against the cultural grain and share personal vulnerability. However, once taken, the risk almost always pays off; authenticity begets authenticity, and a control trap, once sprung, loses its power for a long time.

LEAD FROM THE HEART, FOLLOW WITH THE HEAD

One high-leverage, relatively low-risk method to unlock control traps is to coach top executives in communication patterns that lead from the heart.

If I were to compile a composite of all the speeches I have heard executives present to layoff survivors, it would go like this:

> Our ROI has eroded to the point where the security analysts have expressed concern over the value of our stock to the shareholders. As you may know, our gross margins have also been declining over the past six quarters and reached a point last quarter where we suffered a pretax loss. Based on recent market research, we have confirmed the fact that we are losing market share in the U.S. and are facing increasingly stiff competition in

Europe. The quality indicators we installed last year
show that we are not making the gains we had planned,
and our revenue per employee has declined. We have
no alternative but to implement a downsizing effort at
this time if this organization is to remain a viable economic entity. It is a straightforward economic decision.
Any questions?

Of course, there are no questions, and the shell-shocked victims shuffle, glassy eyed, back to their desks.

All the points in this typical speech are valid causes for
downsizing. However, it is a communication of abstract ideas,
and initially, layoff survivors are not ready for "head" communication. They are anxious, fearful, mistrustful, and in crisis, even if they appear controlled or unemotional. They need
to be reached at the "heart" level, not the "head!" Logical,
analytical, rational data do nothing for them. They need something more personal and human.

Managers communicating layoffs are presiding at a funeral, not an MBA class on financial analysis or analytical decision making. Conducting a funeral requires an empathetic
touch, the naming and sharing of a feeling, and a grieving
for our common human vulnerability. Imagine the outrage
and sense of violation survivors would feel if a participant in
a wake for a loved one launched into a fact-filled dissertation
on actuarial tables, mortality projections, and the need for
death in order to prevent overpopulation in the world.

Managers who deal with people in crisis must lead with
the heart and follow with the head. The head is important
too, but people in crisis are not ready for it. They must attend to their emotional needs first, before they will have room
for more cognitive communications. With a little practice,
managers can begin with the heart, not the head. Indeed, they
can often deal with the cognitive issues in the same meeting
if they pay attention to the heart first. The change from head
to heart is a high-leverage change; a small amount of effort
will lead to a large gain in authenticity and empathy. I have

often been humbled when, after what I perceive as sophisticated interventions, clients tell me that the one thing I did that helped the most was to teach them the "simple" heart-head timing of communication.

If the executive's speech announcing layoffs had begun with the heart, it would have sounded like this:

> I know you are feeling sad and concerned about your friends who had to leave. I know this because that's the way I'm feeling too. It is really hard to see people who have helped build this organization get laid off! I've talked to some of you, and I know you're anxious about your own future and concerned that you may also have to go. I'd like to be able to assure you that won't happen, but the fact that I can't foresee the future and honestly make that commitment makes me even sadder. These are tough times and things are not easy for any of us. I think we are all going to have to struggle through and make the best of it. It helps if we can be honest and share our feelings. Ultimately, it will help if we can move the organization to be leaner, more flexible, and market focused. It is sometimes helpful for me to think of the forces that cause us to have to resort to layoffs. Our ROI has . . . "

HEART AND HEAD LEARNINGS

It is easy for organizational leaders to see and feel the power of the heart and head approach. It is often more difficult to convince them that they have the skills to use this approach and that it is all right for them to share their feelings openly with employees.

The examples of the layoff speeches illustrate three main points.

■   The approach of leading with the heart and following with the head is a model for all survivor interactions. Survivors are in crisis. Acknowledging their underlying emotions is a necessary first step for any meaningful communication.

■   Heart-head communication liberates the sender as well as the receiver. Organizational leaders who share their feelings before retreating to analysis experience the cathartic effect of authenticity.

■   The risk is worth the reward. A small gain in using and communicating feelings can reap large rewards for managers. This is a high-leverage intervention.

TELL THE TRUTH
AND NEVER SAY NEVER

George was a general manager for a semiautonomous research and development division of a large West Coast–based corporation. Many of his division's engineers and technicians were in their mid-forties. They had been with the division for a long time, many since college, and like their organization, they were slightly out of date. Most of them were now in administrative or quasi-management roles.

All the hooks of the old employment contract were operational. The organization was the primary social outlet for many employees through a network of company-sponsored recreational activities such as softball, golf, and bowling leagues; social activities such as dinner dances and trips; and a number of special interest clubs. Most of the old-timers had grown up together in the division and formed friendships there. The fringe benefits were great, much better than the market, and the pay was high for the work done. Even the new engineers, of whom there were too few, were already in a codependent relationship with the organization.

Turnover was very low, thus payroll costs increased each year, even though productivity did not increase, and the margins of George's division continued to decline. The old employment contract was performing admirably, acting as a magnet, pulling the employees in, causing them to define themselves in terms of where they worked, not who they were. At the same time as they were being drawn in by the old contract, they were coming closer to the new reality. The division was merely drifting along, with a market advantage created by an earlier patent breakthrough. The result was predictable: a violation of the old contract and devastating layoffs!

The men and women in this organization, both survivors and victims, displayed various cultural trinkets with pride. During the exit interviewing process, nearly every male victim was wearing his gender's version of the organization's tenure trinket: a tie bar coded silver for five years or gold for ten years, with various colored stones inserted in the center for further five-year increments. The preferred tenure trinkets for women were either key chains or earrings, and many women also continued to display these trinkets. It is a sure sign of the strength of the old employment contract when layoff victims wear trinkets designed to celebrate tenure on their way out the door!

This division had all the preconditions for layoff survivor sickness, and it was no surprise that the division was experiencing early symptoms. George was developing authentic communication, the primary Level 1 intervention. He had a strong desire to tell the survivors that the downsizing was over. The pressure on him to make this reassuring statement was enormous. His direct reports were saying, "We've done the hard things, made the cuts, got the work force down to where it should be. Let's tell them it is over, and get back to work." A related theme was "*They* can't go through that again; *they* need to hear it's over," which meant that the management team really wanted George to tell *them* it was over! (This form of projection occurs often with top managers.) In fact, everyone, at all levels of the organization, wanted to hear it was over so that they could go back to the old ways. The desire to turn back is a natural reaction to change, threat, and uncertainty. Children want to travel back in time during loss or hurt, nations want to turn the clock back during economic or social flux, and organizations suffering layoffs want to be told the downsizing is over, that things can go back to the way they were.

George may also have wanted to tell himself the layoffs were over, even though deep down he knew they weren't. So, despite my advice (and I was not suffering George's tremendous stress and anxiety), George told employees the downsizing was over. He did a lot of other things right. He talked to the employees in groups, and thanked each group for their courage, acknowledged their fears and survivor feelings, and owned up to his own feelings. He then talked about the new vision. This was good stuff. However, he committed that fatal mistake made by many organizational leaders; he told them it was over! He also used the old "if only" theme: if only you work hard, embrace the vision, are more customer focused, and embrace quality, if only you do these things, we will have a bright future together, and there will be no layoffs. I could see a physical relaxing, and almost hear the sighs when the groups heard this. The boss was a hero! He said no more layoffs. Things will be better; we can forget this nightmare. He said we wouldn't have to go through it again!

At one level, no one really believed it. The employees were all intelligent adults and knew what forces were at work in the world economy. But on the public level, they were reassured, or at least had a shared fantasy of the kind everyone buys into at some time in his or her life: the boss said it would be okay. Work hard and you will get your reward. The bad guys never win. Vote for me and the economy will turn around and there will be no tax increases. Racism and sexism do not really exist in my city. The predictable happened. Six months later, there was another round of layoffs and George, the hero boss, became the villain and is now working hard to regain his lost credibility.

TRUTH-TELLING LEARNINGS

The example of George's mistake illustrates three profound points for organizational leaders to brand into their memories.

- Leaders feel tremendous pressure from all parts of the organization and from within their own psyches to say, "It is over!"

- It is never over! This is as close to a law as anything I have found in the study of layoffs. The forces of the economy, the dynamics of technology, and the reality of the new employment contract make any kind of a long-range employment promise an illusion.

- Telling oneself and other survivors the truth takes tremendous courage, foresight, and tough love. The truth is the exact opposite of what survivors want to hear. Nevertheless, layoff survivors need to take individual responsibility for their job security and face the probability that they cannot count on their current jobs to last. In the articulation and understanding of this truth lies the path to a more authentic, less codependent employment relationship.

TWO DENIAL TRAPS

For best results, Level 1 interventions must be planned before layoffs actually occur, and be implemented during the reductions or, at most, thirty days after these reductions begin. After thirty days, survivor symptoms solidify, and the path to healing becomes steeper and more difficult to traverse. But Level 1 interventions are often blunted by management's denial of the validity of survivor problems. By the time organizational decision makers begin to see the depth of the issues, too much time has passed and process interventions have lost much of their potential effectiveness. In some organizations, denial is so entrenched that nothing is ever done, despite overwhelming evidence of survivor sickness. Some of these organizations have failed. Some are dead but have not realized it. Although denial exists in most organizations, it can be overcome through external intervention, the courage of an individual manager, or awareness (one of the purposes of this book). However, management faces two *denial traps* that can confound the situation.

Denial Trap 1: Spurious Self-Actualization

A medical technologies firm whose specialty medical device had captured a large percentage of a narrow market niche had grown from less than thirty to just over five hundred employees in less than six years. At about the same time as the competition caught up with this firm, a number of quality problems surfaced in the firm's cash cow product. Sales declined, earnings were depressed, and the venture capitalists who had originally bankrolled the company became nervous. The firm had had one minor layoff in its manufacturing operation and was planning a large and comprehensive "restructuring."

The firm's human resource vice president was serious about wanting to "do it right," and invited me in to help with the planning of process issues. She believed she was acting in accord with the desires and objectives of her boss, the president. It was clear that the employees were deeply concerned, fearful, and anxious about the future. The members of the top team had been selected for their technical skills, not their management or leadership skills, and communication, which had been tenuous in the best of times, had virtually ceased in the past two months.

The first clue that a denial trap existed in the form of spurious self-actualization was that neither the president nor any key staff member was willing to take the time to talk with me. They were too busy, out of town, or had conflicting meetings. This, to a consultant, is always a sign of resistance and suggests that the top team may not be serious about dealing with the issues. The human resource vice president organized a time to discuss layoff planning and the restructuring during the top team's weekly staff meeting. The meeting revealed a turned-on team. The chief financial officer was deeply involved in seeking new funding alternatives, and the manufacturing vice president was studying new processes and a number of subcontracting options. The president was looking at a strategic alliance and was in the early stages of a mating dance with a merger partner. The organization was in a crisis, and the top team was playing save-the-company. They were fatigued, tired, and stressed, but they had never felt so challenged or relevant! They had a feeling of self-actualization, but this fulfillment would turn out to be spurious.

When I told them the rest of the organization was slipping into the initial stages of layoff survivor sickness and that they needed to do something about it, they responded that they didn't have time. They wondered why they could not delegate that "soft" stuff to the human resource people. (As a result, I fired myself as this organization's consultant.) Nine months later, the "merger" became recognized as an acquisition, and the organization was in dire straits. A few months after that, the president was fired, and the organization became a small division of the acquiring organization.

Spurious Self-Actualization Learnings

- There is frequently a gap between the activities of top management and of the rest of the organization. In times of crisis, top managers engage in the exhilaration of playing a save-the-company or save-the-division game. They may feel almost messianic in this mission. In the heat of the challenge, they have little empathy or understanding for the rest of the organization.

- Spurious self-actualization is widespread in organizations.

- Spurious self-actualization is short-term and delusionary. It is based on the macho and isolationist (and typically American) principle that a small group or an individual can "save" a large number of others. But no one can save an organization attempting to hide behind the old employment contract (the market will see to that), and the days of the Lone Ranger riding in and saving the town are long gone. Collaboration, human bonding, and teamwork are the tools that save modern organizations, not a separation of the top from the rest of the organization.

Denial Trap 2: Myopic Mergers

Many layoffs are triggered by mergers. In a description of useful prescriptions to combat post-merger survivor sickness, Mitchell Marks and Phillip Mirvis (1992, p. 18) point out that survivor sickness "infects employees even in the best of deals." In my experience too the myopic merger denial trap is often a complicating factor in survivor sickness. There are ten homely working principles that illustrate why the attitude that 'they'll leave me alone; I'll leave them alone" is a denial trap:

- The difference between an acquisition and a merger is control.

- The organization that has the control calls the transaction an "acquisition."

- The organization that does not have control calls the transaction a "merger."

- The acquiring organization has a built-in compulsion to install its people, systems, and policies in the acquired organization.

- The acquiring organization often denies its nature, fights against its compulsion, and promises autonomy.

- The acquiring organization eventually follows its compulsion!

- The merging organization colludes with the acquiring organization and buys into the promise of autonomy.

- Deep down, the merging organization knows it will be taken over, its systems replaced, redundant people laid off, and identity diluted.

- Both the acquiring and the merging organizations are deeply psychologically invested in maintaining their mutual denial.

■ The primary intervention in these situations involves straight talk and honest communication within and between the two entities.

It is very important for organizational leaders to work through this interlinked denial trap. Although most post-merger layoffs occur in the merging organization, there are cases where survivor symptoms have bled over into the acquiring organization, usually owing to a long and confusing series of false starts in the relationship. Bleed-over is minimized when quick, decisive planned action and communication take place. Before this can happen, management must take the time and have the honesty to develop a clear joint vision and implementation plan. Unfortunately such honesty and time taking is a rare occurrence.

PROCESS RESEARCH

Much of the fledgling survivor research has focused on process issues (factors that have an impact on survivors and can be managed before, during, and shortly after layoffs) as opposed to longer-term individual and systemic solutions that might provide a more permanent immunization to layoff survivor sickness. This research has also tended to be laboratory-based studies of controlled student populations and extrapolations from other theories as opposed to field-based, face-to-face interactions with survivors in their workplaces. Nonetheless, it is an important and growing body of knowledge that supports field-based studies and practitioners' experience. The major themes in this process research are survivors' needs for fairness, equity, participation, caretaking, and prior notification.

Fairness
Like beauty, what is fair is often in the eyes of the beholder. Therefore, the perceived fairness, not only of the reason for

a layoff but also of the process for selecting those who leave, is an important hygiene factor for survivors. The practical implications of this survivor need are, once again, that communication must be clear and honest. Open discussions are needed about the layoffs' rationale about the way layoff selections were and will be made. The key ingredients are trust and authenticity. Without the lubricant of trust, layoff processes will grind out anger and fear and polarize groups within the organization.

Equity

Do the layoffs include top management? What is the difference between their exit pay and the severance of the average middle and lower manager? Survivors are concerned about sharing the burden. Layoffs that include a disproportionate percentage of middle managers and "workers" exacerbate normal survivor symptoms. Even if the number of layoffs is fairly distributed across the board, severance equity will remain a major concern. Newspaper reports and proxy statements that tell of multimillion-dollar payments to departing top executives leave survivors feeling abandoned and outraged.

Participation

Did the organization consider alternatives: voluntary retirement, special severance bonus payments, full-time changed to part-time or to job sharing, pay freezes and cuts, or long-term leaves of absence? In a laboratory experiment, Jeannette Davy and David Tansik (1986) applied the concept of procedural justice to layoffs. Procedural justice allows individuals to have input into the outcome. They found that people were more satisfied when they were given control in establishing the conditions of a layoff—such as the process of choosing who will be laid off, amount of time required for prior notification, and amount of severance pay—than when they had to choose between predetermined options. Such participation is rare in real organizations owing to distrust and management's need for control. However, those are not insurmountable barriers. I know of two organizations that put similar ideas into operation. A large manufacturing operation actively involved employees in exploring alternatives to layoff, and a relatively small service business involved employees in establishing criteria for those who would be laid off. In both cases, it took courage and conviction on the part of one employee to bulldoze these ideas through a resistant system.

Caretaking

The way layoff victims are treated is a survivor hygiene factor. Their severance pay, efforts to help them find other employment, and the dignity and respect granted them by the organization are parts of this factor. Horror stories such as rumors that victims have been told of their fates by a secretary when the boss is out of town or, worse, by a human resource person whom they have never met, go through survivor organizations with amazing speed, whether the stories are true or not. In one division of a large organization, stories were told of layoff victims' being given no advance notice, asked to clean out their desks, and then escorted to the human resource function where they were "read their rights," given a severance payment, and escorted to the door by a security guard. Indeed, these incidents did take place, but in another division two years earlier! There is power in management's publicizing what is being done right, and great harm, for many years afterward, in management's tolerating practices that rob layoff victims of dignity.

Prior Notification

The longer the advance notification the better. Public corporations in the United States must work within the constraints of the legal issue of materiality. Corporations with material news that will affect the price of their stock must make internal and external announcements of this news simultaneously. However, many organizations take secrecy far beyond this constraint. Well after an initial public announcement in divisions far from corporate headquarters, organizations will remain concerned that layoff rumors are leaking, and that these organizations often maintain elaborate security, holding secret meetings and formulating elaborate need-to-know communication plans. This intricate web of secrecy is based on assumptions about negative employee reactions, not on Securities and Exchange Commission concerns.

Enlightened practice would argue that the longer employees know in advance, the more they are put in control, can plan their own futures, and are able to face and manage their own anxieties. Companies argue that employees who know too much in advance will spend all their time looking for jobs and will not be productive. The fact is, once layoffs are announced, the survivors' focus will shift from the job to their survivor symptoms in any case, and without preparation and adequate notice the shift will be much *more* intense and substantial rather than less so.

Ethics is also an issue here. A manager who knows that he or she is going to do something "to" another person, who also knows that advance notice would be helpful to that person, and who nevertheless withholds that notice for purposes other than strictly legal ones is not going to win the ethics in business award.

Finally, most organizations have a key constituency that requires advance notice. These are the employees the organization wants to keep. They may be high potentials, key managers, or key technical employees. They need to hear that management values their contributions and will do its best to keep them. This needs to be said in the right tone, with the right disclaimers. Managers do not know for sure that they can keep anyone, and if they are honest, they do not even know about their own longevity. They can, however, communicate intentions.

Middle managers who will be asked to administer the layoff also require advance notice. They are the implementers, who should not be too far removed from the planners. The layoff timing, numbers, and processes and the communication process all need the ownership of this group.

LEARNINGS AND IMPLICATIONS

Layoff processes have important effects on survivors. Authenticity, congruency, and empathetic communication are primary Level 1 interventions. All of us—top executives, middle managers, and individual contributors—erect traps to control and manage the information and emotions that should be spontaneous and free flowing. In order to be relevant to ourselves and our fellow survivors, we need to go against the grain and resist our tendencies to control and deny. We need the courage to engage in straight talk with ourselves and others.

Dealing with survivors' perceptions of fairness, equity, and caretaking, and permitting prior notification and participation in decision making are other important Level 1 interventions.

Process interventions are tactical. Though important, they are hygiene factors that serve only to stop the bleeding; they do not promote healing. Healing itself begins with emotional release, or grieving. Second-level, grieving interventions are explored in the next chapter.

8

Level Two:
Facilitate the
Necessary Grieving

"Some of the people are ushered out of here
coldly, like it's all over and you can't even say
goodbye to your friends. They come in here
and clean off their desks at night. All of a
sudden, the desk is clear; it's gone. They've
disappeared."

Level 2 interventions unblock
repressed feelings. Even in the best-handled layoffs, survivors
feel violated. They must release their feelings before they can
go on. Since organizations often have strong norms against
employees' even admitting the presence of survivor emotions,
let alone sharing and dealing with them, second-level interventions frequently must tease out repressed emotions. While
some survivors avail themselves of private therapy and others
have support systems that allow them to sort out their feelings,
the vast majority of layoff survivors repress their feelings and
have no personal or organizationally sanctioned outlet for

anger and fear. The metaphor of the surviving children is once again instructive. Imagine the energy the surviving family expends to repress their strong and toxic emotions and go about their daily routines. Unfortunately, organizations too are filled with survivors slogging through endless bleak days, repressing their feelings of violation, and as their anger turns inward, sinking deeper and deeper into the funk of survivor guilt and depression.

The bad news is that repressed anger and other emotions are so widespread. The good news is that the intervention process is not difficult to start, and once it is started, the feelings do come out. Initially, the organization may have to use outsiders to start the process. In the long term, management should integrate a process for facilitating survivor grieving into the organizational system — experts leave, reductions continue. Although individual counseling and therapy are useful, I have found group work the most effective and efficient method of bringing survivor emotions to the surface. This chapter presents case studies from my consulting practice to illustrate Level 2 interventions.

A "FAMILY"
GROUP INTERVENTION

The client. A director of support services in a recently merged health care system, and her surviving managers.

The situation. Two large hospitals merged. Sarah's unit was responsible for providing central services such as accounting, computer, training, human resource, records, and maintenance services, and a number of other administrative and technical services, for the new organization. Before the merger there were two managers for each of these services; after the merger there was only one survivor. Not only had many managers lost their jobs, the remaining organization was rightsized, which meant another 20 percent reduction in Sarah's department. Nearly nine months after the layoffs, the productivity and morale of the group had declined to the point that it was clear to Sarah that the group was suffering from what I have called layoff survivor sickness.

The intervention. Sarah and her "family," the group of survivor managers who reported to her, participated in a three-day retreat with the objectives, which they stated in health care language, of "diagnosing and developing a treatment plan" for what ailed them.

The retreat started at noon, and by dinnertime, with the aid of the metaphor of the surviving children and other exercises, some participants began to express their survivor feelings. Everyone was then given an assignment of writing his or her survivor story. Story ground rules required the use of feeling language and a personal focus — escape to abstraction was not allowed. The next day, with a great deal of facilitation and support, the managers told their stories; first individually, then combined with the stories of others in small groups, and finally as part of the entire family story. Before the merger, both hospital systems had self-perception of being kind and nurturing. However, the story that emerged at the retreat was a sad one, filled with blaming and perceptions of betrayal.

That day was filled with tears, anger, and touching occurrences of emotional support. Over dinner that evening, the intervention switched from the heart to the head. The group viewed a slide show of the symptoms of layoff survivor sickness. The participants were then split into two groups and given an assignment to develop a one-act play, a tragedy based on the class story.

The next morning, the groups presented their plays, which turned out to be more humorous than tragic (this shift seems to be typical in similar groups). Then they spent the next few hours discussing how their efforts could be turned into inspirational plays. Sarah, who had previously been either a participant or a silent observer, led this discussion. In the early afternoon, two new groups were formed, with instructions to write and act out an inspirational play that could serve as a new vision for the team. These two plays were presented after dinner with Sarah as the "judge," armed with several humorous prizes. The plays had humor, power, and passion. Sarah, overjoyed and somewhat tearful, told the groups that the performances "knocked her socks off." (I have seen several versions of this exercise and am always amazed at the participants' creativity, intensity, and optimism.) Sarah told the group they never could have done this without the "agony" of the past two days.

The next morning, the entire group talked about ways of transferring the learnings to their organizations, established some ground rules as to how group members would relate to each other back home, and planned two future meetings.

"FAMILY" GROUP INTERVENTION LEARNINGS

■ In a relatively short time most natural work teams, or "families," can make a great deal of progress in unblocking and addressing their survivor feelings.

■ Because of the importance of having someone involved who knows how to deal with feelings in a positive and productive way, this intervention should not be attempted without an initial diagnosis, a supportive boss, and a skilled facilitator.

■ Often survivor feelings must be teased out through metaphor, structured exercises, and nontraditional processes such as drama.

■ Layoff survivors express powerful and passionate feelings easily when given the opportunity. Conversely, survivors' suppression of these feelings takes an enormous toll on productivity and on simple human authenticity, day after day, week after week, and often year after year.

■ Interventions must deal with the head *and* heart *and* feet! "Mono–body part" events have poor results. Working at the emotional level (heart) is extremely important, but if overdone, alienates participants. Working only at the cognitive level (head) is also important, more so than many behavioral practitioners realize, but if overdone, it also alienates people. Action planning, doing something with what has been learned (feet) is a priority for busy managers. But action with no emotion or theory behind it is a self-delusion. Unfortunately, it is a delusion that many action-oriented managers use to avoid or to sabotage real learning.

- In successful group interventions, the extent to which even sophisticated and psychologically hip leaders and managers are reluctant and ashamed to own up to their own survivor feelings is often experienced as a collective "Aha."

- Nearly every group, even one working over a very short time frame, yearns for a galvanizing vision. For this reason groups should seek a new vision even in their early getting-the-feelings-out cathartic sessions.

- Participants and facilitators must take symbolic survivor feelings literally. The exercise of developing and performing a play is a literal acting out or purging of survivor feelings.

- Facilitators should involve the "family" head. Sarah's team must continue to function when the outside facilitator is long gone; therefore, it is important not to create any dependence on the outside. (Although transference and, if the outsider is not careful, counter-transference often do occur, even in relatively short sessions such as the one just described.)

- One-shot cures do not work. Even when they have fully positive immediate results, short-term fixes do not take. Sarah had a strategy of multiple sessions. There are always ups and downs in multiple sessions too — the earth did not move at all of Sarah's subsequent sessions.

A SYSTEMWIDE INTERVENTION

The client. The new CEO of a spin-off division of a high-technology communications company.

The situation. As a part of a corporate restructuring, a large product organization spun off a specialty division. The former division general manager became the new operation's president and CEO. In order to make this operation show sufficient short-term profit to satisfy the demands of the venture capitalists who helped fund the spin-off, an across-the-board work force reduction of about 10 percent took place just before the formal spin-off. Six months later, another substantial layoff took place. At this point, the vice president of human resources convinced the top management group that a systemwide intervention to "revitalize" and "recruit" the work force was needed to pull the new organization out of its continuing decline.

The intervention. The initial step was an "off-site" for the top team. In the new president's words, the team's objective was to "plan" ways to "increase the productivity" of the work force. (Language is a lens to a culture — the health care organization had a "retreat" to "diagnose" and develop a "treatment" plan; the business organization went "off site" to "plan" an increase in "productivity.") The results were far less dramatic than those of the health care group. There was much denial; the president was particularly resistant, often becoming directive and outspoken and stifling dialogue. However, the team's survivor feelings did get discussed, and the tragedy plays yielded insights for the president, as both groups portrayed him as the archvillain. On a scale of ten, this intervention would rate a five. That score is about par for the first time a top team goes through this kind of session because the higher the organizational level, the greater the denial, and the greater the difficulty of staying out of the head and in the heart.

The next step was a series of one-on-one meetings with the top team members. As any change agent will agree, it is

crucial that systemwide change have ongoing top management involvement. I continued to help individuals vent their
emotions during these sessions. Team members had a great
deal of anger at the parent company for spinning them off
with no choice. They also blamed the president for "selling
them out" and for bad leadership, each other for not pulling
an equal amount of weight, and the employees in general for
not following directions, for failing to be "grateful" that they
had a job, and for not appreciating the extent to which team
members were working their "ass off to meet the payroll." The
president was disturbed by the feedback he had heard, and
he blamed the top team for not understanding his vision. He
also was anxious to "do" something and was impatient with
me and my internal colleague, the human resource vice president, for not implementing his ideas to increase productivity
and "raise morale."

The third step was another meeting with the top team.
Originally scheduled for one afternoon, it lasted nine hours.
This was not a popular meeting. Most consultants occasion-
ally reach a point at which they must take a stand, and I was
prepared to abandon the project if team members did not
face their own issues before attempting to "do" something
"to" the rest of the employees. Team members had received
copies of Harvey's Eichmann sermons (Chapter Three), and
the meeting started with lots of argument and a high level
of affect. (Harvey's sermons are guaranteed to evoke a strong,
usually negative initial reaction from top management.) After that they heard the collected themes from their one-on-
one meetings: the anger, the blame, the hurt that employees
did not recognize top management's efforts to save the business, and the institutionalized anxiety that they were ineffec-
tively attempting to escape through a quick-fix orientation.
This time, they were able to both own and work their data.
By the time they adjourned, they had not only made an initial pass at dealing with the group's layoff survivor symptoms
but had also formulated a systemwide intervention strategy
that was to be integrated with the management structure. The
integration involved the following steps.

- Require all managers to attend a "revitalization" work-shop. Managers were to attend in "stranger" groups, rather than in groups with managers working for the same supervisor. First, this workshop would help the managers to examine and confront their own survivor feelings. They then were trained, or often refreshed, in basic helping skills: listening, giving and receiving feed-back, and responding to feelings.

- After managers attend the workshop, require them to meet with each of their employees, focusing the discussion on the layoffs and asking about employees' feelings. (Managers would have an outline and a structured check-list to facilitate this discussion.) Even though many managers were not experienced in conducting such inter-views, the top team felt that the managers were the natural organizational communicators and that any discussion of survivor symptoms, regardless of how clumsy, was infinitely better than no discussion.

- Plan a communication and team-building program to take place over the next year to build commitment to the new vision.

The program got off to a positive start. However, less than three months into implementation, the president was let go by the board, which included venture capitalists. The new CEO promptly instituted another round of layoffs, in which one of the top management team's key supporters of the program was let go. After that, the program simply fell apart for lack of funding and support.

SYSTEMWIDE INTERVENTION LEARNINGS

- Systemwide interventions are difficult to sustain within organizations experiencing significant flux and change.

Coalitions and management support do not hold together over time.

- Survivor groups should be met where they are, not where the intervener wants them to be. The initial language and intervention strategy need to be formulated in a way survivor groups will understand and accept. Confronting them in the first ten minutes with their repressed survivor symptoms and blaming behavior will only get the external intervener thrown out and leave the layoff survivors without any help.

- A time comes, however, when the intervener must confront survivors and, in order to help them, run the risk of losing them.

- Involving line managers is the only natural way to implement a systemwide intervention.

- Something is better than nothing! Even though some line managers are not gifted at teasing out survivor symptoms, others are. Even the most awkward management intervention can have a positive effect. Help is defined by the helpee, not the helper, and employees suffering from survivor sickness seem appreciative if anyone tries to help.

- Even limited success makes a difference. Some groups in this organization are still working on survivor issues.

A DEPARTMENTAL WAKE

The client. The corporate human resource department of a defense contractor.

The situation. The defense contractor had suffered continuing significant layoffs over a three-year period. When the vice president of human resources left, the new vice president differed in values and education from her subordinates. Margaret had a Ph.D. in counseling psychology and had worked in education prior to joining the company. She was also the company's only woman at the vice presidential level. Margaret quickly diagnosed her department as "burned-out" and unable to "let go of the past." In this case, the past had included high growth, lots of "fun" projects, and for the industry, relatively high job security. Margaret wanted her team to move from a controlling, "rules administration" role to a "helping" role; she wanted her group to perceive employees as "clients."

The intervention. After I held a series of diagnostic interviews and small *discovery group* sessions, it was clear that members of this department did indeed have a death grip on the past and were extremely angry about organizational changes and their diminished role. Those who had spent time conducting exit interviews and dealing with layoff victims' pay and benefits engaged in the rationalization and justification behavior described in Chapter Six.

The initial intervention for this department was a version of the family workshop. Due to a large degree to Margaret's sensitivity and group-process skills, this was a very powerful and helpful session, both in terms of expressing emotions and of identifying a new vision. One successful activity that evolved during that session and that I have used successfully in other organizational settings was a departmental wake, culminating in an actual burial.

Rather than participate in the small-group plays described earlier, the entire group decided to hold a wake, complete with candles, music, and testimonials. Individuals wrote out the old-system ideas and activities they needed to let go of, read their lists, tore them in half, and placed the torn-up paper in a large cardboard box draped in black. Then each person, including Margaret, stood in front of the group and read from a list of his or her fears. This list too was torn up and placed in the box. Some people "said words" over the box. Although this has not happened in other groups, Margaret's team joined hands around the box and sang "We Shall Overcome." The session ended when the group symbolically buried the box by putting it in the dumpster behind the conference center. (Once another group actually buried the torn slips of paper in a vacant lot beside the group's facility.)

This intervention and others that followed had dramatic

results. The organization bonded around a new image of service and, with Margaret's continuing facilitation and support, successfully navigated a number of wrenching changes.

DEPARTMENTAL WAKE LEARNINGS

■ Symbolic acting out has power and value. Even organizations that initially perceive this exercise as strange and "touchy, feely," find potency and meaning in it. My most resistant group reported this exercise as the most meaningful when they looked back three months later. At some level, the burial is real, and the wake, like its real-life counterpart, serves as a symbolic way of letting go of the past and allowing survivors to move forward.

■ Confession is cathartic and bonding. Team members stood in front of their peers and owned up to a wide range of survivor feelings. People learned to their surprise that others harbored the same set of feelings. Therefore, the process of confession led to sharing and acceptance. Survivor feelings were accepted as a natural consequence of what individuals had been through.

■ The intervention is easier when the boss has good interpersonal and group-process skills. When bosses are less skilled in human relations than Margaret, the process is more labored and needs more outside facilitation. However, the results are still positive.

■ Organizational survivors easily make the connection between the grieving process and their survivor symptoms.

EMPOWERING LEADERS THROUGH MODELS OF CHANGE

The case studies in this chapter are not intended to present an unchanging methodology but to illustrate the wide number of options and latitude for creativity available to interveners. Interventions can be facilitated by helping professionals or skilled managers from inside or outside the organization. However, because internal managers and staff are also survivors, who are part of the system and who, at times, are in codependent with the system, initial interventions typically work best when done in partnership with an outsider. In addition, Level 2 interventions should not be started without diagnosis of the organizational culture and of the depth and breadth of layoff survivor symptoms. If line managers play roles in the intervention, they should have guidance from a trained helping professional.

These caveats do not mean that organizations should forever rely on outsiders for Level 2 interventions. To the contrary, such reliance on forces outside the system to solve the system's problem creates an unhealthy dependency and disempowers managers. The need for Level 2 interventions is so widespread that the best gift an outsider can give any organization is the capacity to continue the process long after the outsider has ridden off into the sunset. One natural way organizations accomplish this transference is by developing a cadre of trained internal interveners. Usually these internal consultants will come from the organizational development or human resources function.

Although empowering these staff groups to solve survivor problems is very helpful, a second level of empowerment is necessary to complete the job. This second level of empowerment comes into play at the interface between employee and boss. The most effective Level 2 work takes place at this interface. Two straightforward interventions are of great assistance when an organization wants to spread helping skills throughout the natural management structure: train managers in the helping skills that are relevant to their new-paradigm role and give them a model for grieving.

Helping Skills

Ask any old-paradigm manager and, sadly, many of today's business schools to define the manager's role and their description will usually be some combination of the trite and dusty "-ings" of the machine age: planning, organizing, directing, coordinating, and evaluating. Most of these old-paradigm managerial functions involve data that can be generated by a computer and handled directly by the employee without any management interaction. The real role of managers in the new paradigm is helping. Managers with basic helping skills are powerful tools in a survivor work force. No one likes to be directed, organized, coordinated, or controlled. When these things are done "to" employees, they turn around and do them "to" someone else. The result is a manipulative, codependent work force bonded around everything but good work. Level 2 interventions require helping, empowering, coaching, and listening skills. I am always amazed at the rapidity with which line managers (even those who see themselves as bottom-line oriented, hard-boiled, or tough-minded) can learn and use basic helping skills (Figure 8.1). A helping skills workshop for all managers and organizational reinforcement of new-paradigm skills and behaviors through the performance appraisal and compensation systems can be powerful tools for ushering in new-paradigm behavior.

A Model of Grieving

Consultants perform an important transference intervention when they help organizations develop the internal capacity to facilitate survivors' catharsis and grieving. Consultants should also give organizations a good theory or model to support their work with survivors. In my early work, I was oriented

**Figure 8.1. Changing Old-Paradigm
"-ings" to New-Paradigm "-ings."**

From		To
Controlling	⟶	Helping
Evaluating	⟶	Empowering
Directing	⟶	Coaching
Planning	⟶	Listening

toward skills and not theory. I thought managers were more interested in "doing" than in theories of why they were "doing." Since then I have discovered the power of Elizabeth Kübler-Ross's model of the stages of grieving (Kübler-Ross, 1969), and I have learned that managers like theories and models.

The Kübler-Ross theory both legitimizes survivor feelings and provides a common language for facilitators and survivors to use when they discuss previously repressed survivor feelings. The Kübler-Ross model has five stages:

1. Denial

2. Anger, including rage, envy, and resentment

3. Bargaining

4. Depression, which includes sadness, gloominess, pessimism, guilt, and feelings of worthlessness

5. Acceptance, which is not equated with happiness

The Kübler-Ross model presents a frame of reference that many managers find useful for understanding and legitimizing survivors' grieving processes. In the following list I have connected Kübler-Ross's stages to the experiences of layoff survivors and layoff victims, in order to help interveners stimulate head and heart communication.

Layoff Victim	*Layoff Survivor*
Stage 1: denial	Stage 1: denial
"It can't happen to me."	"That's the way businesses operate."
	"I'm not a victim, not emotionally involved."
Stage 2: anger	Stage 2: anger
"It's not fair."	"I can't act out my feelings of anger."
"I can't act out my anger and rage."	
"I resent those who stayed."	"I feel guilty and angry that I remain employed."
	"I feel separated—I'm a victim too."

Stage 3: bargaining
"I'm better than some who
are staying—keep me."
"Can I get longer notice
or better terms?"

Stage 4: depression
"I feel sad and pessimistic."
"I'm not worth keeping."

Stage 5: acceptance
"I'm cut out of the
system."

Stage 3: bargaining
"How can I negotiate my
own safety?"
"Can we look at options
other than laying off my
colleagues?"

Stage 4: depression
"It's bound to happen to
me sooner or later."
"I've lost my joy in work
and spontaneity."

Stage 5: acceptance
"I'm not the same—I've
been violated."

LEARNINGS AND IMPLICATIONS

Today, most layoff survivors are suppressing strong, toxic, and debilitating survivor emotions. Level 2 interventions help survivors express these feelings and get them out on the table so they can be dealt with. Emotional release and the necessary grieving over the layoffs and a lost way of life are prerequisites to healing. Facilitating the release and the grieving is a key management role.

In order to help others organizational leaders must first help themselves. They must confront their own survivor feelings and get past their natural repression and shame. They must discover that it is okay to feel bad, that survivor feelings are a natural consequence of old-paradigm conditioning carried over to the new reality. But it is not right for anyone to avoid dealing with survivor sickness. Repression of survivor symptoms is hazardous to individual and organizational health.

Dealing with repressed survivor feelings and facilitating grieving is not the end of the intervention process. But the catharsis that occurs during Level 2 interventions is a milestone along the road that will lead to individuals' breaking organizational codependency and becoming self-empowered. Third-level interventions, which will help individuals reach this goal, are the subject of the next chapter.

9

Level Three: Break the Codependency Chain and Empower People

"It isn't necessarily a commitment to the company; it's a commitment to the kind of work that I do. So it's a commitment to my own self, and it's a commitment to my department, too, but not necessarily a commitment to the company."

The purpose of third-level interventions represents a basic shift in focus from earlier interventions. Levels 1 and 2 react to existing layoff survivor symptoms. Level 3 offers the possibility of preventing the sickness in the first place. Level 3 interventions are both more complex and more hopeful than Levels 1 and 2. They are complex because, in the final analysis, they are played out within each person's human spirit. They are optimistic because they have the potential to help people move from being victims to being adventurers in control of their own identity, happiness, and creative powers. The field of codependency research and treatment offers both a language and a frame of reference that can help managers and employees understand how to bring about this optimistic transformation.

DAGWOOD TAKES A STAND

On Sunday, September 6, 1992, millions of Americans awoke to find new-paradigm behavior unfolding in the comics of their morning paper. After more than fifty years in an abusive, manipulative relationship, Dagwood Bumstead, the prototypical old employment contract employee, walked into his boss's office and standing tall, with fists clenched and a resolute expression, told Mr. Dithers that he was quitting! Not only was he quitting, he was going to work for his wife, Blondie, in her catering business. What may have seemed one small step for a cartoon character was a giant leap forward in symbolic terms. Dagwood had broken the chains of organizational codependency.

Art does imitate life, and this could not have happened ten or even five years ago. Back then, those of us who had our early values and stereotypes about gender roles and the nature of the employment contract shaped in part by Dagwood, Blondie, and Mr. Dithers would not have understood. We would have rebelled. It was evidence of the new paradigm's strength that we now accepted and, yes, admired Dagwood's stand.

Cartoonists Young and Drake also illustrated something beyond the obvious easing of the old stereotypes and their unnecessary limitations. They showed the personal courage an employee must have to break out of an employment relationship that is hazardous to his or her self-esteem and personal authenticity. When Dagwood Bumstead got mad as hell and wouldn't take it anymore, he not only walked away from the J. C. Dithers Company, he walked away from organizational codependency and toward personal empowerment. That, I suspect, is why many of us cheered him. Alas, two weeks later, we opened our Sunday papers and found our hero had fallen. He returned to J. C. Dithers Company, crestfallen, having been fired by Blondie for eating the catering business's profits.

Dagwood's brief flirtation with empowerment demonstrates three realities of organizational codependency: (1) risk taking and courage are necessary to break out of a codependent employment relationship, (2) it is easier to become empowered than to remain empowered, and (3) codependency is a disease in and of itself. Dagwood, as a personality archetype, is hard wired to be a permanent victim.

ORGANIZATIONAL CODEPENDENCY

Third-level interventions help individuals break organizational codependency and lead a self-empowered life. When individuals are self-empowered and have personal control of their self-esteem and sense of relevance, they are immune to layoff survivor sickness.

Codependent behavior is ancient. One could say that it started in the Garden of Eden. However, the label and the formal concept date only from 1979 (Beattie, 1987). The initial, relatively simple idea was that people who deny their feelings, alter their identity, and invest a great amount of energy in the attempt to control an alcoholic share the alcoholic's addiction; they are codependent with the alcoholic. The idea has now been expanded to cover many other forms of addiction, and codependency is considered by some to be an underlying, primary disease in itself (Schaef, 1986). Just as a person can exist in a codependent state with another person in relation to an addiction, a person can also be codependent with an organizational system. People who are organizationally codependent have enabled the system to control their sense of worth and self-esteem at the same time that they invest tremendous energy attempting to control the system.

People are the "carriers" of organizational codependency. The network of organizational codependency can be visualized as a series of chain links, from bottom to top and across all levels, as though a chain-mesh fishnet covered the organizational pyramid, with each link a reciprocal codependent relationship. The people in these relationships are ensnared in a collective Abilene Paradox: they are all conspiring to be collectively something that they do not want to be individually.

Relationships that are free of unhealthy control and dependency are fun, spontaneous, and creative. The same is true of organizations. Organizations that are free of codependency are vibrant, open, and productive. They are filled with employees who are invested in good work and managers who are competent in helping skills. Although they too may have layoffs, their survivors are largely immune to survivor sickness because the survivors (and those laid off) do not index their self-esteem and sense of personal worth to the organization, but rather to their own good work. Layoff survivor sickness is dealt a double blow in these organizations: employees are virtually immune because they are not unhealthily dependent, and the organizations tend to be much more productive and competitive because employees' immunity frees up employee energy and creativity. Thus, the incidence of layoffs is reduced.

A primary symptom of codependency is that the codependent's sense of value and identity is based on pleasing, and often controlling, not himself or herself but someone or something else. Codependents make themselves into permanent victims. People suffering from layoff survivor sickness are similar full-time victims. Survivor symptoms are caused by survivors' surrendering to organizationally imposed values and organizationally imposed identity. The primary Level 3 intervention brings about the effort that will break this codependent relationship.

Breaking any codependent relationship is a struggle requiring a personal act of courage. That is why we admired Dagwood Bumstead's effort. Even though he failed, he tried

to rid himself of what — despite the humor and stereotyping —
in real life would be an unhealthy and manipulative employment relationship. Blondie too made and implemented a courageous decision when, over Dagwood's earlier protestations,
she started her own business. I hope Blondie and Dagwood
hang around the cartoon strips for another fifty years. It will
be interesting to see how they fare. Living free of any form
of codependency is a lifetime effort. Each individual's goal
is to live life as an adventurer and not as a victim.

To break the organizational codependency chain, individuals must maintain internal control, keep their personal power,
and love themselves without making this love conditional on
organizational approval. They must maintain their authenticity, without obsessively and schizophrenically attempting
to both please and control the system. The organizational goal
is empowered employees working with minimal control. They
work because they are invested in the task and interested in
a quality product, not because they need to control or please
others to maintain their self-esteem. Like individuals' efforts,
organizations' efforts to maintain a culture that allows empowerment and shuns codependency must be unending.

Several common codependency treatment strategies can
be effectively translated into Level 3 survivor intentions. Those
strategies are detachment, letting go, and connecting with
a core purpose.

DETACHMENT

In codependency treatment, detachment is a facilitating
strategy. Without detachment the codependent cannot take
actions that promote personal autonomy and healing. In classic codependency treatment, the object of this detachment
is the addicted other. Codependents must detach themselves
to the point where they no longer index their self-esteem and
identity to the behavior of this other. Detachment is also
necessary to break organizational codependency. If who you

are is where you work, you will do almost anything to hang on. If employees derive their sense of identity, self-esteem, and uniqueness from pleasing the boss and remaining in an organizational system, they are in an organizationally codependent relationship. They have given up their uniqueness; their focus and energy are external, artificial, and bent on pleasing.

Good Work

The concept of good work is essential to an organizational detachment strategy. Good work always starts internally. It is the outward manifestation of internal gifts and talents. Even in an organizational environment, good work is goal driven, not relationship driven. The purpose of good work is to produce something or to accomplish a task, not to please the boss or impress the system. Pleasing the boss or impressing the system may happen as a consequence of good work, but these consequences are not good work's primary intent. Good work is a basic component of the new psychological employment contract, which is short term and task oriented. When Paul Hirsch (1987) calls for "free agent management" and advocates self- as opposed to organizational loyalty, he is advocating what I call the new employment contract. Because this contract is grounded in good work, not in pleasing relationships, it promotes detachment. Conversely, because it was grounded in relationships and pleasing, the old psychological contract stimulated codependency.

The Seductiveness of "Person Capturing"

Organizations of the past have been very good at sucking the autonomy from employees and fostering institutional codependency. The seductiveness of the process is illustrated by the budget presentation of a human resource director in an old employment contract organization that was just beginning to feel the irrevocability of the new paradigm.

Brenda began by outlining a number of the strategies the organization had in place to meet the "continuum" of employee "needs." These strategies included benefit plans, recreation programs, group travel benefits, day care, tuition reimbursement plans, and a comprehensive "career planning" system. Brenda concluded her presentation with the statement that these strategies served to "tie the employee to the organization over the long term" and helped to "capture the total person." However, this organization's difficulty was that it had already captured too many people and tied them in too well. It needed to untie many.

"Person capturing" is an old-paradigm strategy. For example, "career planning" in Brenda's organization took a long-term view of employees. Career paths had been laid out by the organization during its days of stability and predictability. However, because employment in the new paradigm is neither predictable nor stable, this organization's career planning was irrelevant to the new reality. Worse, the implied promise of long-term planned careers had created employee dependency. The implied promise had been effectively shattered during the heavy layoffs that had recently plagued the organization. However, organizations typically hold on tenaciously to the assumptions in the old contract long after their utility has disappeared. The idea of holding on to employees in order to be prepared for a predictable future is seductive and hard to shake. Despite its recent layoffs, Brenda's organization approved her budget and the old strategy carried on for one more year, even though the real need was for management to communicate the impending reductions and develop strategies of detachment that would enable people to take individual control over their career planning, rather than trust that vital task to an institution.

Diffuse Root Strategy

Despite increasing evidence as to the disutility of the old strategy, many organizations continue to delude themselves, and many of their employees, by attempting to "tie in" employees. In these cases, the employees must untie themselves.

The detachment process begins with an individual's decision not to rely on an employer to nurture all aspects of his or her life. The basic change that must occur can be most easily illustrated by comparing two plants. One plant can get all its nourishment from a taproot, just as an employee's self-esteem, identity, and social worth can all be nourished by a single organization (Figure 9.1). When this is the case, the codependent will manipulate, cajole, control, and scheme simply to hang on. Considering the option, manipulating and controlling make sense. What happens if that single taproot gets cut? If who you are is where you work, what are you if you lose your job?

Another plant may have a diffuse root system, reaching out to different areas of soil. Emotionally healthy individuals reject the simplicity and seductiveness of having all their needs nourished through a taproot into the organizational soil.

Figure 9.1. Taproot Strategy.

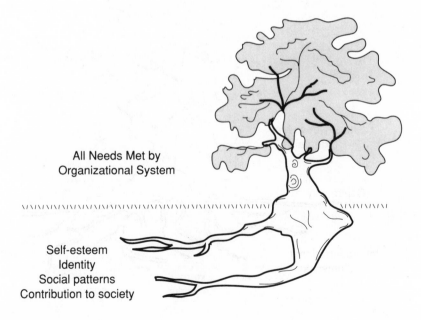

All Needs Met by
Organizational System

Self-esteem
Identity
Social patterns
Contribution to society

Through planning and effort they develop a diffuse root system (Figure 9.2). They establish a nondependent relationship, so that if the organizational root is cut, they can still function, grow, and thrive. It is simple and effective for managers to ask employees to diagram their own root systems. Many employees are surprised to find that they have a virtual taproot into their organization. Their discovery can serve as a wake-up call and stimulate them to cultivate other options, and diffuse roots.

Although detachment is a primary intervention in all codependency, achieving detachment is a continuing battle for many. As I mentioned, one view of codependency (Schaef, 1986) is that it exists both in relation to a specific situation, alcoholism for example, and as a disease in itself. This means

Figure 9.2. Diffuse Root Strategy.

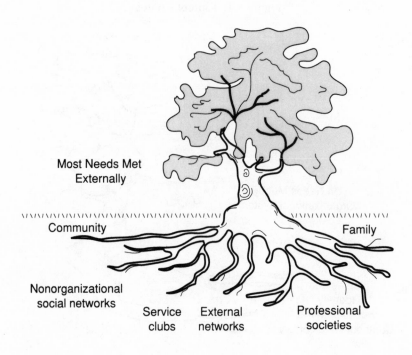

that those with the illness of codependence, if left untreated, will go through life moving from one codependent situation to another. Dagwood went back to Mr. Dithers, and we have all seen employees who seemed to have broken the codependency chain move into organizational situations that have restored their codependency. According to Anne Wilson Schaef, both the specific situation and the underlying disease must be treated. Level 3 interventions deal with the specific codependency situation. However, since employees spend the majority of their waking hours in working situations, these interventions may also contribute to the solution of the underlying disease.

LETTING GO

Codependents feel compelled to control others. "We nag; lecture; scream; holler; cry; beg; bribe; coerce; hover over; protect; accuse; chase after; run away from; try to talk into; try to talk out of; attempt to induce guilt in" the other person (Beattie, 1987, p. 69). When they are controlling another's behavior codependents often operate outside of reality. If you are a codependent, you will try to "force life's events to unravel and unfold in the manner and at such times as you have designated. Do not let what's happening, or what might happen occur. Hold on tightly and don't let go. We have written the play, and will see to it that the actors behave and the scenes unfold exactly as we have decided they should. Never mind that we continue to buck reality. If we charge ahead insistently enough, we can (we believe) stop the flow of life, transform people, and change things to our liking." (p. 71).

Again and again in my practice, I see employees at all levels desperately trying to retain control of a decaying and nonproductive work environment. They are often consumed in acting out a play that closed long ago. The old employment contract is dead, and holding on to it is toxic to human spirit. Despite this reality, workers and unions continue to

cajole and demand job security and higher wages for un-
changed work and productivity. Middle managers set up elaborate control systems to artificially maintain managerial influence in the face of computing and information technology
that makes managers' link-pin, information exchange role
outdated. Top managers cling to fantasies of organizational
permanence and long-term decision making. During crises
such as layoffs, controls are intensified, information is managed, the truth is feared, and straight talk is driven underground by control talk.

The paradox of codependency is that the controllers are
always controlled; that is what makes them codependent. The
alcoholic dances a control dance with the codependent other,
but the alcoholic always leads! Organizational codependents
are ultimately controlled by the organizational system. The
more they try to turn back the clock, manage the natural flow
of honest information, ignore the facts in favor of an artificial
reality, or suppress their own needs and feelings, the more
they dance to the very tune they are attempting to control!
They become focused on controlling reality rather than helping the organization be productive within the real world.

Organizational codependents need to let go, to admit
the folly of their attempts to control an uncontrollable situation. They must trust their own perceptions. This puts them
in a bind. Codependents tend not to trust their perceptions
unless they are validated by someone else (Schaef, 1986). However, because codependent organizations are made up of interlocking webs of codependent relationships, and no one in
these organizations trusts his or her own perception about
the emperor's lack of clothes, validation is hard to come by.
That is why the nondependent outsider, or an insider with
the courage to speak his or her mind, is often the one who
breaks the logjam. In fact, speaking what to an organization
is the unspeakable is often what the organization perceives
as the best use of an outsider intervener's skills. I call this a
straight-talk intervention. Such interventions do not always
work, but when they do they are dynamite! An example of

the liberating power of straight talk took place at a firm I will call XYZ Company.

Straight-Talk Intervention

The top management team of XYZ, a small professional organization, met one weekend at a resort to work on a strategic plan, which they visualized as a formal document that would be distributed to all their employees. The organization had had a significant revenue shortfall due to losing a large contract. The members of the top team were contemplating a significant "cutback" of professional staff, even though they prided themselves on never having laid people off in the past. Prior to the meeting, the top team engaged in abstractions and speeches on the subject of the lost contract, but team members did not discuss what the organization was going to do about the revenue shortfall. When I pressed the issue during pre-meeting interviews, the conversations grew strained and stilted.

During the morning of the first day of the planning meeting, the team members developed an elaborate procedure to outline their external and internal environment, formulate their "driving force," develop a series of strategic goals, relate the goals to their mission statement, and draw up short-term action steps. On the surface, they were working well and doing a good job of developing a traditional strategic plan, but the event had an artificial feeling, like a play with bored actors going through the motions.

That afternoon it was clear that something was fundamentally wrong. The group had no energy, the plan was just a series of words on flipcharts, and no one had dealt with the revenue shortfall. When the group reconvened after dinner, I confronted them with straight talk. I fed back the themes of the pre-meeting interviews and my observation that some norm was preventing people from talking about the immediate financial problem and that the meeting thus far was a victory of form over substance. I asked, "Why is it not okay to discuss this issue?" I was persistent, but what was even more important was that, beneath the surface, the group wanted to get the issues on the table.

Eventually, there occurred what a group member graphically called "squeezing the boil." The issues all came out, as he said, in "one gooey wad!" The trigger was one person taking a risk, having the courage to speak his mind and to tell the truth. His straight talk revealed a number of issues that were creating group paralysis. The managing partner was new in his role, did not know what to do, and was afraid of looking bad to his colleagues. He was so consumed with controlling his image and hiding his fear that he simply repressed the financial issue. The others, knowing there would have to be a reduction, were protecting their own staffs. They did not want to raise the issue and be the ones to trigger the cutback. The administrative vice president was afraid for his job and felt sure that if there were reductions the nonprofessional staff would be the first to go. The culture of the organization was conflict averse and nonconfrontive. Essentially, the top team was just hoping that if it controlled the organizational reality the problem would go away!

Straight talk begets straight talk, and by the end of that planning meeting, team members had come to grips with their revenue issue, giving each other honest feedback for the first time and beginning the long and painful path toward authenticity and letting go. Shedding covert control needs is not a one-shot proposition, and this management team is still in process after holding a number of what the members now call "straight-talk sessions." The company did experience a small layoff, but the top managers were able to deal with their bottom-line issue primarily through stringent cost control, including a salary cut and a bonus moratorium for the top team.

"If Only"

The career of an industrial/organizational psychologist exemplifies the way an individual codependent holds on to codependency. Edith had emerged from a midwestern Ph.D. program as a classic "dust bowl empiricist." To her, there was no knowledge except that which could be quantified, statistically analyzed, and measured. Her need to see the world in terms of predictable and therefore manipulatable data points predisposed her to the control orientation that was to paralyze her later in her organizational life. After a brief flirtation with academia, she went to work in the human resource function of a large organization. It was a traditional old employment contract organization, still in the growth phase, unaware that disaster was waiting just around the corner. Edith became the "queen" of measurement. She did test validation, performance management studies, employee attitude surveys, training evaluation studies, and anything else that could be quantified, measured, and reported to upper management. When the first round of layoffs hit, she was managing a small group of three other psychologists and a support staff of five.

Edith's boss was abusive, sexist, and took personal credit from top management for much of her excellent work. She spent a lot of energy managing (controlling) her relationship with him through a wide range of controlling behavior: denying what was happening, telling him what he wanted to hear, hiding the abusive relationship from her staff by only meeting with him one-on-one and threatening to go to top management unless he changed.

She also controlled her staff and her colleagues. She was a perfectionist, wanting all her reports in a format and context predetermined down to the color and size of the paper. When she worked on cross-functional task forces, she wanted people outside her function to understand her data the way she understood it and was frustrated if they came to other conclusions. She spent much energy attempting to control their interpretation, often through overwhelming them with data. She played the "if only" game: if only they had enough information they would react the way she wanted them to react. She did not see this as a question of whether they could have their own opinion. For her, it was simply a process of moving them to the "correct" conclusion—hers!

Edith's top management interactions were also marred

by the if only game. When some executives, in order to avoid Edith's data overload, requested Edith's employees to make reports, she "coached" the employees in ways of controlling interpretations, thus killing two birds with one stone; she overloaded and controlled her subordinates and top management at the same time.

Her reaction to layoffs was an extended if only game. She entered into a massive internal advertising and public relations campaign designed to communicate the message, "If only you understood the good things I am doing for the organization, you could come to no other conclusion than to retain me and my staff!" Her boss, colleagues, and top management received reports, charts, graphs, personal presentations, all to suggest her irreplaceability. When, despite her efforts, she was ordered to "terminate" her support staff and all but one psychologist, she redoubled her efforts to prove her value. When the inevitable happened and she too was "taken out" of the organization, leaving only her former subordinate in place of her entire department, she was shattered.

The happy ending of this story is that Edith's termination served as her wake-up call. Through a combination of therapy, career counseling, and an ongoing support group, Edith has come to grips with her codependent control needs. Now a partner in a very small consulting firm, she considers herself "a recovering codependent."

Letting-Go Learnings

The examples of the XYZ Company and Edith are by no means extreme cases. They exemplify the common holding-on behavior found in most organizational systems. There are six learnings from these examples.

- Not telling the truth, repressing reality, and holding back feelings and perceptions is a form of denial. These controlling behaviors actually shift control from the self to the other (in those examples, to an organization). These behaviors are contagious and, as illustrated in the XYZ example, can result in a collective disavowal of reality. If unchallenged, they can result in organizational failure.

■ Truth telling is a powerful letting-go intervention. It usually is an act of individual courage since it often violates a strong cultural norm. Truth telling too is contagious and frequently results in freeing up people's energy, so that they can deal with fundamental organizational issues.

■ Attempting to control others so they do what the controller wants them to do or be what the controller wants them to be, as opposed to what they want to do or be, is a futile and manipulative effort. Its predictable results are a movement of control from the would-be controller to the other; the loss of personal power, autonomy, and self-esteem; and the interminable and draining investment of energy to control the uncontrollable.

■ Controlling, whether through denial (repressing individual perceptions of the truth) or through overt manipulation (attempting to induce others to think, do, or act the way the controller want them to), is a major cause of organizational codependency and increases susceptibility to layoff survivor sickness.

■ Letting go of the need to define oneself through others' behavior and reclaiming individual control of self-esteem is the major antidote for self-destructive control needs. Letting go is not easy. It requires constant struggle, feedback, and support at both the individual (Edith example) and organizational (XYZ example) level.

■ Letting go is an act of faith. It is often terrifying. As crummy as things are, at least you know what they are! A venture into the unknown has been compared to moving through a series of trapezes. In order to maintain momentum, you have to let go of one and have faith that there will be another to take its place. There is a terrible moment of fright when you have let go of the old, and the new is not yet there to grab hold of. Such is the nature of personal growth. If you do not let go, you will have absolute control, but you won't go anywhere. You will be hanging, alone and isolated, in control but hollow and separate. If you take the leap of faith and let go, you will continue to move, you will still be in process — there is always another trapeze out there — but you will have the adventure of recapturing your destiny. It is a paradox with no respite on either side. Letting go frees you to grow, but growth forces you to accept a continuing disequilibrium. Holding on offers predictability, but you cannot hold on forever. Eventually fatigue will cause you to drop into the void of continued codependency. It is far better to undertake the adventure, frightening though it may be.

CONNECTING WITH A CORE PURPOSE

The third set of organizational codependency immunization activities involves tapping into a core purpose. This is a powerful yet elusive quest, for it is a spiritual journey. In traditional codependence parlance, this is the Twelve-Step Program, originally developed for alcoholics. It requires the recovering person to surrender and give himself or herself over to a greater power. The twelfth step reads, "Having had a spiritual awaking as the result of these [eleven previous] steps, we try to carry this message to alcoholics, and to practice these principles in all our affairs" (Beattie, 1987, p. 189). Today, the Twelve-Step Program is used in treating all manner of addictions, including codependency. The program has a natural position in the flow of third-level interventions: individuals must first detach, then stop controlling, and finally, awaken to unifying purpose and identity. Detachment and letting go involve removal; connecting with a core purpose involves a putting back.

Connecting with an underlying purpose or mission has a spiritual dimension that may or may not be formally religious in nature. Each person must determine his or her unique purpose in life. In many organizations, this purpose is difficult for people to discuss since these organizations have norms against talking about spirituality or personal meaning. Since most organizational leaders now realize that business organizations are the social systems in which people spend large parts of their lives, these norms are unproductive holdovers from the old paradigm. Part, perhaps the most essential part, of the human condition involves our quest for meaning and relevance in the universe. To assume that we set aside this basic human pursuit when we enter the workplace is to deny a basic reality.

Don't Place Your Spiritual Currency in the Organizational Vault

Under the old paradigm, a great deal of people's sense of relevance and purpose was provided by the organization, which behaved somewhat like a religious institution. A small consumer finance organization that had been acquired by a larger financial services institution is a good example. There was a hierarchical all-male "priesthood" that culminated in a charismatic founding father who was deified by the employees and who responded by dispensing gifts (a year-end bonus and promotions) to the loyal. This organization had its catechism in the form of a belief system that customer service was supreme and a demand that personal needs be subordinated to an overarching organizational loyalty, with the ultimate reward of continued employment and the honor of being part of the team.

This organization had other characteristics of a formal religion: a regular Saturday morning meeting (service), with stories of sales and quota achievements followed by applause, handshakes, and affirming smiles (testimonies), and a pep talk by the founding father (sermon). There were rewards (gift certificates for dinners for two dispensed to some who had done an extra good job) and symbols (a watch commemorating fifteen years' membership in the congregation). The organization did not have a company song, but it did have a number of mottos and slogans, tacked to office walls. I learned some things they did not teach me in graduate school from this organization. First of all, this structure worked! It did not feel contrived. The organization was highly productive and efficient. Second, the organization was essentially a spiritual place. Employees derived a sense of purpose, worth, and value from it. Unfortunately, because the organization was newly acquired, it then experienced a layoff and was the unwilling recipient of a number of policies and procedures that stripped away its uniqueness.

That, of course, is the moral of the story. It is not healthy to place one's spiritual currency in business organizations' vaults. The organization cannot guarantee that currency's safety. This view of the organization as a religious system is not limited to small firms with a hands-on, charismatic leadership. IBM is an example of a more abstract hierarchical religious institution. Although it did have a company song and still has revival meetings (100 percent clubs), the spiritual bond it once had with its employees is cracking, and the congregation is confused.

People need more personal, more secure, and less organizationally dependent sense of purpose or spirit. This does not mean that they cannot or should not attempt to find meaning or purpose within business organizations. It does suggest that the origin of an individual's purpose and spiritual meaning ought to start within the individual and spill out into organizations. Purpose should not be a property of the organization, flowing from the organization to the employee and conditional upon continued "membership."

The pilgrimage to seek personal meaning and purpose does not lend itself to prescription. However, the pilgrimage is often started by a "wake-up call." Wake-up calls may result from layoffs as well as from other of life's attention-getting devices—heart attacks, deaths of people close to us, and divorces. Such intensely emotional events cause people to ask deep and searching questions. For this reason, the trauma surrounding organizational unraveling provides excellent teaching and learning opportunities. The following exercises are of value in seeking a core purpose.

Core Purpose Exercises

- *Write a personal mission statement.* Individuals can also be asked to share their statements with significant others both in and out of the organization. This sharing results in feedback, provides a reality check, and stimulates communication. Individuals often find great value in this experience. For example, one manager had his wife and children sign his mission statement, which he now displays in his office.

- *Develop a lifeline.* Individuals prepare graphs outlining their personal highs and lows from birth to the present and then project this lifeline to their projected date of death. They must also predict cause of death. People are always amazed at how few good years they have left. Next they outline what they want to accomplish during the remaining years. Sometimes, they write their own obituaries and have others read them. This is a serious, introspective, and powerful experience that often leads to clear values and basic spiritual insights.

- *View the organization as religious institution.* Following a discussion of symbols, artifacts, and belief systems, individuals write a story of their organization as a temple, synagogue, mosque, church, or any other formal religious structure. Afterward, they examine the degree to which they derive spiritual satisfaction from the organization and then write another story in which they are "excommunicated." Alternatively, they can be asked to pick the

symbols, rituals, and belief systems that are most important to the organization, and to imagine what would happen in a takeover by another religion with opposing belief
systems and rituals.

■ *Define good work.* In this guided imagery process, participants explore what for them, and uniquely for them,
constitutes good work. They explore periods of extreme
joy in work, work spirit, and personal satisfaction; contrast these experiences with opposite experiences; and
attempt to distill the core components of their personal
good work.

Exercises such as these are short-term, relatively "canned"
experiences. By themselves, they will not provide a long-term,
fundamental sense of purpose or individual mission. They
can, however, stimulate the quest for this purpose. Organizational survivors take these exercises seriously and achieve an
impressive depth of self-discovery in a relatively short period
of time.

Regardless of how this third component of breaking organizational codependency is accomplished, it is at the heart
of the personal empowerment that prevents layoff survivor
sickness. Possession of a personal sense of purpose and mission enables employees to retain internal control and accomplish good work in their lives, regardless of organizational
boundaries.

LEARNINGS AND IMPLICATIONS

Organizational codependency is seductive. It is the outcome
of fifty years of organizational strategy designed to tie employees in for the long term. It is easy to be lulled into a pattern of pleasing and controlling. We must have the courage
to engage in detachment, to stop defining ourselves in relation to our business organizations, and to resist the simplicity

of putting a taproot into organizational soil. We need to let go, to stop controlling and manipulating the system. Above all, we need to connect with something bigger than ourselves, with a personal core purpose. The result will be a rebirth of spirit, self-control, and a work relationship centered on good work, as opposed to manipulation and control.

Breaking organizational codependency is essentially an individual effort. The individual detaches from the organizational system as a culture. Organizations too need to detach, let go, and discover their core purposes. Organizational struggles mirror individual efforts, and it is difficult for organizations to detach from their paternalism. Moving away from employee control and toward true employee empowerment means letting go of an attitude rooted in history. Searching for a new purpose and vision in the face of global competition and world economic parity involves the pain of creating a new identity. However, for both individuals and organizations the gain is well worth the pain. The pay-off is survival and relevance in the new paradigm. Reformulated organizations have the opportunity to create systems and processes that are congruent with the new employment contract and to form a new partnership with empowered employees who have broken the chain of codependency. This partnership is the subject of the next chapter.

10

Level Four:
Build a New
Employment Relationship

*"I am committed to my customers. I am
committed to the people who use my
services, and it doesn't make any difference
where I work; it's the people that I work with
that I really enjoy, and I really want to do a
good job for them."*

Level 4 interventions create
systems and processes that structurally mitigate layoff survivor
sickness. These interventions grow out of the new psychological employment contract. (Tables 10.1 and 10.2 outline
the implicit assumptions, strategies, and outcomes of the old
and new employment contracts.) The old psychological contract was forged in the post–World-War-II culture, where big
was better, relationships were long term, and the United States
enjoyed a historically derived competitive advantage. Today,
many of the old contract's assumptions and strategies are
played out against far different realities. The resulting mis-

Table 10.1. Old Employment Contract.

Implicit Assumptions (Based on Old Environment)	Strategies	Outcomes (Based on Current Environment)
Employment relationship is long term.	Benefits and services that reward tenure Employee recognition processes that reinforce long-term relationship	Older work force Demographically narrow work force
Reward for performance is promotion.	Linear compensation systems Linear status symbols Fixed job descriptions Static performance standards	Plateaued work force Demotivated (betrayed) work force
Management is paternalistic.	Excessive and duplicative support services Long-term career planning systems	Dependent work force
Loyalty means remaining with the organization.	Approved career paths only within the organization Voluntary turnover penalized Internal promotion; discouragement of external hiring	Narrow work force Mediocre work force Nondiverse work force
Lifetime career is offered.	Fitting in Relationships	Codependent work force

Table 10.2. New Employment Contract.

Implicit Assumptions	Strategies	Outcomes
Employment relationship is situational.	Flexible and portable benefit plans Tenure-free recognition systems Blurred distinction between full-time, part-time, and temporary employees	Flexible work force
Reward for performance is acknowledgment of contribution and relevance.	Job enrichment and participation The philosophy of quality Self-directed work teams Nonhierarchical performance and reward systems	Motivated work force Task-invested work force
Management is empowering.	Employee autonomy No "taking care" of employees No detailed long-term career planning Tough love	Empowered work force
Loyalty means responsibility and good work.	Nontraditional career paths In/out process Employee choice Accelerated diversity recruiting	Responsible work force
Explicit job contracting is offered.	Short-term job planning Not signing up for life No assumption of lifetime caretaking	Employee and organization bonded around good work

match leads to conditions that foster layoff survivor sickness. The shift from the old to the new contract affects all organizational members. Those who manage and lead share the same confusing environment with all other employees. No one is to blame for the shift, which is complex and requires both organizational and individual accommodation. Organizations and individuals must now behave in accordance with a new reality that runs contrary to values conditioned into us over a long period of time. The differences between the old and the new employment contracts is best understood as a series of shifts from what was to what is.

FROM A LONG-TERM TO SITUATIONAL EMPLOYMENT RELATIONSHIPS

Organizations operating under the old contract assumed employees would be there over the long haul. As I described earlier, organizations rewarded tenure with strategies from tie bars and wall plaques to recreational services and benefit plans. Today, organizations are reaping what they have sown. Because of the success of these strategies in establishing long-term commitment, many companies now have an aging, non-diverse, locked-in work force. The middle and upper management ranks of many old-paradigm organizations are populated by disillusioned old white men. That this situation is inadequate is not anyone's fault; it is the outcome of demographic, cultural, and worldwide competitive changes.

Walter Tornow and Kenneth De Meuse (1991), among others, have aptly stated that the ties that bind have become very, very frayed. Organizations operating in the new paradigm do not need an aging, locked-in work force. They need just the opposite: a flexible, diverse, and situational employee population.

From the employees' perspective, being tied in is confining and no longer feels comfortable. Employees feel trapped by health insurance plans that cannot be duplicated or afforded outside the organization and pension plans that have a heavily weighted pay-off for employee longevity. Many employees are locked into organizations that do not want them and where the employees do not wish to remain. What are needed are systems compatible with the new reality.

Flexible and Portable Benefit Plans

People's need for adequate and affordable health insurance that is not tied to the place where they work requires a change in U.S. national policy. This change is a priority, both for the health of U.S. citizens and for the efficiency and competitiveness of U.S. organizations. Although pension plans are portable in some professions — education, for example — pensions remain a difficult and complicated issue, one that tends to lock in rather than free up employees. Government and private sectors must cooperate if we are to solve the problem and develop flexible and portable benefit plans.

Tenure-Free Recognition Systems

Revamping recognition programs is something organizations can accomplish without government assistance. Even though it makes no sense to celebrate employees' tenure in an organization attempting to be situational and flexible in the way it employs people, the idea of changing organizational symbols and rituals is hard to sell in organizations where top management has risen up through the ranks and has a great deal of cultural identity invested in honoring tenure. Nonetheless, looking for events to celebrate that are more consistent with the strategy of the new employment contract is a very important intervention. It is a relatively small effort with the potential for a large pay-off because changing organizational rituals is dramatic and makes a strong statement about the new culture. Here are three suggested changes.

- *De-emphasize and, if possible, discard inappropriate trinkets.* Tie bars, cuff links, bracelets, wall plaques, and other public symbols that celebrate employee tenure give the wrong message when an organization requires a flexible, situational employment relationship. (Employees in one organization tell the survivor horror story of a well-liked production supervisor who received her ten-year bracelet on a Monday and was laid off that Friday!)

- *Celebrate achievement.* Catch people doing things right and find a way to publicly reinforce their achievement. There is nothing wrong with using trinkets, dinners, theater tickets, or simply public pats on the back as rewards, as long as they celebrate desired behavior. New employment contract organizations find ways to celebrate goal ahievement, excellence in customer service, and good work. They do not have a use for unauthentic relationships based on pleasing others, nor do they value time spent in the organization.

- *Celebrate departures.* Under the new employment contract, an employee's leaving is a cause for celebration, not lament. If the organizational goal is a just-in-time work force, one that is situational and available when appropriate good work is needed, the organization will have a continuing flux of arrivals and departures. Leaving will be a planned event, a celebration of achievement. The leaving ritual should be more than just a quiet departmental lunch. It should be an organizationally sanctioned event and a rite of passage.

Blurred Distinctions Between Full-Time, Part-Time, and Temporary Employees

Many old employment contract organizations built walls and made clear distinctions between various categories of employees. Full-time, so-called permanent employees were at the top of the scale, and temporary part-timers were at the bottom. When the organizational goal is a situational employment relationship, the strategy has to develop a much more fluid work force. Today in some organizations, it is impossible to tell whether an employee is a "temp," a "contract," a "part-time," or a "full-time." This is the trend of the future. Evidence of the demand for the flexible employee is the growth of contract employment firms and temporary help agencies that fill both traditional clerical and newer managerial and technical temporary jobs.

To develop a truly flexible just-in-time work force, organizations must remove artificial pay, benefits, and status distinctions among employee classifications. Given what has been happening in many organizations for the past ten years, full-time permanent employees are a rare and endangered species. All employees are now temporary, and artificial status, pay, and benefit differences based on how temporary employees are do not fit into the new paradigm. Organizations that continue to maintain sharp differentiations between employment categories not only cut themselves off from a growing and fresh source of new people and ideas, they put unnecessary barriers in the way of the crucial flexibility they need for future survival.

FROM REWARDING PERFORMANCE WITH PROMOTION TO REWARDING PERFORMANCE WITH ACKNOWLEDGMENT OF RELEVANCE

A fundamental old-paradigm assumption was that the basic reward for employee performance was promotion. In reality, many organizations used promotion to reward factors other than performance, such as loyalty, fitting in, and length of service. Under the old employment contract, organizations developed compensation systems that were hierarchical in scope and linear in design. The way to get more money was to get promoted. Status symbols such as office size, reserved parking spaces, and accessibility to special dining areas were also linked to employees' hierarchical levels. Job descriptions were linked to levels and, in classic Weberian bureaucratic fashion, were arrayed hierarchically, like a pile of blocks. Performance standards, in turn, were linked to these static job descriptions. There was nothing inherently wrong with this arrangement. It served organizations well, given conditions of continued growth, advantages to being large, and long-term predictable planning horizons.

The world, however, has changed. To survive in this new world, organizations are shrinking, accepting short-term planning horizons, demanding employee flexibility, and becoming nimble and responsive to global changes. New-paradigm organizations have flattened, or delayered. As Bardwick (1986) has pointed out, promotions in these flatter firms are far and few between, and a large percentage of the work force is structurally plateaued. This plateaued work force feels betrayed because it was taught the old-paradigm assumption that promotion is the reward for performance, yet organizations cannot deliver on this promise. Promotion was the currency of the old realm. The new realm offers task investment, job enrichment, participation, and a shared vision. The outcome of this new currency is a work force motivated by task investment in good work. There are several new-paradigm strategies that help to create this motivated work force.

Job Enrichment and Participation

Job enrichment is an old idea whose time has come. The clear linear chain of promotions that characterized the old employment contract depended on static jobs but today's organizations need adaptable employees. Organizations should expand jobs laterally, empower employees to make decisions, and form structures to facilitate job enrichment. Job enrichment does not mean simply adding the duties of departed employees to the job descriptions of those who remain; such tactics overwhelm employees and increase their survivor symptoms. True job enrichment eliminates nonessential tasks and *invests* employees in relevant, useful, achievable work. In the new paradigm, the opportunity to do good work in an enriched, participative environment replaces promotion as a motivator. Employee participation could not grow in the soil of the old paradigm, but within the new, it is a key component of empowerment. Good work is accomplished through employee voice and choice.

The Philosophy of Quality

The total quality movement is another concept that could not flourish in the structured, control-oriented soil of the old paradigm. One of the reasons a total quality movement often starts with a flourish but stalls as it approaches the top of the organization is that those at the top often carry the cultural baggage of the old paradigm into the new reality. As the Chrysler advertisements read, "those at the top had better lead, follow, or get out of the way," for the philosophy of quality is a natural fit with the new employment contract. It is necessary to separate the bureaucratic wrappings from the essence of the quality philosophy to appreciate the fit. Total quality is not about programs: slick announcements and slogans, hierarchical checking, and patching quality goals onto the existing system. Measurement is important, but only as a means, so quality is not about Pareto charts and histograms. Customer orientation is a total quality core value, but not just because it provides a service focus. A customer focus also gives an organization a structural immunity to the internal-relationship focus that leads to organizational codependency.

Separated from its techniques, total quality is about empowered people performing good work that serves others. This theme runs through the basic philosophies (as distinct from the techniques) of all the quality gurus. Whether you follow Crosby, Deming, Feigenbaum, Ishikawa, or Juran, the central idea is the same: the philosophy of quality is empowered people, linked together by good work that serves others. And, what is most important, this idea is also the essence of the new employment contract.

Self-Directed Work Teams

Another tool that was blunted by the paternalism and control orientation of the old paradigm is good work performed by empowered family, cross-functional, or nonhierarchical teams. Although a number of good techniques are available to help managers develop and empower these teams (Wellins, Byham, and Wilson, 1991) it is again necessary to separate the techniques from the essence. Self-directed work teams are important in the new employment contract because they require managers to take a helping, facilitating, and coaching role while the empowered teams bond around good work, uninhibited by unnecessary old-paradigm controls.

Redirected Performance and Reward Systems

Organizations must make their performance and reward systems relevant to the new paradigm. This may seem obvious, but in many organizations these systems remain linked to the dying paradigm of the past, a fact that explains the continuing frustration of most managers and employees. Managers need to be appraised and rewarded for new-paradigm behaviors, not old-paradigm control. If coaching, facilitating, helping, and empowering are the tasks of new-paradigm management, the reward system should reinforce these behaviors. *Performance management* describes a number of healthy and productive new approaches that are systemically based and consist of explicit contracting and employee accountability, but the term itself smacks of the old paradigm. *Managing* another person's performance suggests *controlling* that performance. Far better to name it *performance facilitation, performance empowerment,* or even *performance contracting.* The shift in terminology does not mean that new-paradigm performance systems let anyone off the hook. On the contrary, they promote employee responsibility and accountability, and free managers to be creative and strategic.

Nonmanagerial employees should be rewarded for networking, "teamworking," participating, and producing good task outcomes. Task and accomplishment is the name of the game. The time has come to bury trait-rating systems forever! Organizations must now implement compensation systems that may have seemed radical, illegal, or administratively difficult in the old paradigm. Examples include empowering self-directed work teams to set compensation policy for team members, moving away from monthly and weekly pay increments and toward task-specific payments, and implementing group performance appraisals and rewards.

FROM PATERNALISTIC TO EMPOWERING MANAGEMENT BEHAVIOR

Once when I suggested to an organization's management committee that a good start toward the development of an empowered work force would be to undo some of their paternalistic management practices, they almost threw me out of the room. "Who us, paternalistic?" they said. "No way! We're a modern organization; we're into participation and total quality! How can we be paternalistic?" However, as they eventually discovered, they were indeed paternalistic, and paternalistic managerial behavior does not stimulate empowerment. Instead, it has the opposite effect, creating a dependent, compliant work force.

Most organizations do not like to think of themselves as paternalistic, or as a female chief operating officer once retorted, "At least call us maternalistic!" But regardless of the label, the reality is that most organizations take pride in "taking care" of their employees. Employee caretaking was an integral part of the old employment contract and is very difficult to reverse, even in the harsh light of the new paradigm. However, organizations must give up caretaking, because employees taken care of by the organization no longer find it necessary to take care of themselves, and their dependency is hazardous to their health. Dependent employees lose skills they must have to thrive in the new paradigm. The result is akin to the fate of wild animals who are taken care of in captivity and then suffer when they are returned to the wild because they lack the skills to fend for themselves. The difference, of course, is that wild animals cannot take charge of their fate; people can. They can learn or relearn needed skills, and organizations must foster this learning.

The roots of the compulsion to take care of employees go deep into human history. Primitive tribes had clear and binding roles and reciprocal obligations of hunting, food gathering, and providing security. Leaders of early settled groups rewarded warriors with land as the spoils of battle. Medieval serfs pledged a portion of their harvest to the nobleman who took care of them by providing protection and land. This idea of taking care of people in exchange for their loyalty and labor was carried on by the old employment contract.

Both employers and employees now find themselves at an interesting place. Modern power holders and employers are unable to maintain their end of the bargain. Their "armies" are merging and many of their loyal workers are being laid off. History seems to have evolved to the point where the employers are discovering their codependence with an ineffective and artificial system. The belief in the "God-given right" of certain people singled out by their gender, family, or race to rule (or manage) others is eroding, as is the belief in the shackling and growth-limiting obligation to take care of those "less fortunate." An exciting and potentially liberating part of the new employment contract is that all employees can have the opportunity to develop the skills and perspective to take care of themselves, increase their self-esteem, and break the limitations of inappropriate and outdated codependent relationships. Organizations can facilitate this new paradigm by encouraging autonomy, letting employees plan their own careers, and applying the principles of tough love.

Promote Autonomy and
Stop Taking Care of Employees

The first step organizations can take to promote employee autonomy is simply to recognize that the old employment paradigm is in its death throes and that autonomy is the best strategy for both the employee and the organization. Managers who have come up through the old employment contract ranks not only have difficulty perceiving that their behavior is paternalistic but also resist changing the system even after they recognize their caretaking. Thus, the price of their action is often trauma. The top management wake-up call is frequently rung by competitive disadvantage, mergers, and layoffs. There are two key lessons for organizations.

- *Do not condition employees to be dependent.* If leaders expect employees to be responsible adults, they will behave responsibly. Most organizational leaders have experience with teenage children. Teenagers need guidance, they need limits, but most of all, they need trust and independence. And at some point, parents need to let go. This may require a nudge or something stronger, even a push! Just as it is not healthy for families to create unnecessary dependence, it is not in the best interests of organizations to attempt to hold on to employees.

- *Eliminate unnecessary support systems.* As I have stated, health insurance and retirement plans are a burden on U.S. organizations. However, organizations cannot simply abandon these obligations. The government, insurance carriers, pension-funding groups, and employees themselves must take more responsibility in this area. A start has been made through the increased co-funding of health insurance, driven by costs. Also, employees are making more of their own choices about the levels of health care their insurance will cover and the levels they will cover personally. Organizations should also scrutinize other employee support systems. A good rule is that if the community provides the service, the organization should think long and hard before it duplicates that service. For example, employees should not depend on the organization that provides a paycheck also to provide organized recreation such as social clubs and sports leagues. Other unnecessary and so-called no-cost support services involve group purchasing power. These services include group travel programs, co-op purchasing plans, and various organizationally sponsored discount plans. On the surface, there is nothing wrong with these plans; everyone likes to get a good deal. The problem is that they are another link in the dependency chain. Empowered, independent employees will find their own discount plans. Many organizations also actively promote social interaction through employee clubs, organizationally sponsored dinners, family picnics, or other services and events that provide socialization at the organizations' expense and, as it now appears, the employees' hazard.

Resist Detailed Long-Term Career Planning

Organizationally specific long-term career paths are artifacts of the old employment contract. Job planning, not career planning, is the stuff of the new paradigm. In the past, employees wanted to know the experiences and education that would, over a career lifetime, get them to the top of a particular organization. Organizations responded with detailed, often elaborately prepared, graphically illustrated, and professionally packaged prescriptions for the tickets employees needed to have punched to rise to the top. In the new paradigm, organizations are flat, growth is not hierarchical, systems are temporary, and careers are short-term and situational. Detailed long-term career planning makes no sense because organizations can neither guarantee employment continuity nor forecast the situational and rapidly evolving skills needed over a thirty-year career.

Why then do organizations persist in offering internal

career planning? This too is a legacy of the old employment contract. Employees seek comfort in asking for a career prescription. Organizations collude and write one, even though they cannot deliver on it. In the end, such collusion only serves to create false expectations and leads to a lose/lose relationship between the individual and the organization.

The E-Word Demands "Tough Love"

The word *empowerment* carries a lot of emotional and definitional baggage. One human resource executive, concerned about his line managers' reaction to the word's perceived softness, refers to it as the E-word and does not use it during management meetings. His managers do not see the E-word in its true perspective. Without accountability, empowerment *is* just a fuzzy word. But true empowerment is the stuff of the new paradigm. Truly empowered employees are also accountable. One cannot happen without the other.

It requires great courage to accept that control is an illusion and to create an independent, self-reliant work force — an empowered work force! Organizational leaders must have the strength to let go, to replace controlling with coaching. They need the tenacity to tell people what they do not want to hear — that there may not be a long-term career for them, that the future is unclear, that there is no guaranteed permanence in organizational systems. Managers need the coaching skills that empower employees to accept personal freedom, to take self-responsibility, to look for opportunities for good work, to relish the task and not deify the system, and to maintain personal control of their lives and careers.

Empowerment requires tough love. Leaders must show "love" for employees not by caring for them but by believing that healthy autonomous individuals have the capacity to take care of themselves. These leaders must let go of their control needs and require employee responsibility and accountability.

FROM TOXIC FIDELITY TO HEALTHY SELF-RESPONSIBILITY

As part of a significant across-the-board multidivisional layoff, an organization was seeking to lay off one thousand people, primarily professionals and middle managers. The organization was in turmoil, the first stages of layoff survivor sickness had set in, and the members of the top management team were desperately seeking a galvanizing vision to hold onto while the organization as they had known it was disintegrating. In the middle of this chaos, the director of marketing resigned. At the top management meeting to work on the vision, the dinner conversation turned into a group lamentation over the loss of such a key player. It was true that the marketing director was considered a high-potential employee and had high visibility since he was only one level below the top management group; however, there were a number of qualified internal replacements. Nevertheless, people attacked his loyalty: "How could he be so disloyal as to leave the organization during this crucial time? Just think of all this company has done for him!"

The next morning the group was challenged to define *loyalty*, as part of reaching their new vision. The question they faced was, if the organization saw a continuing need to "take out" managers and entire layers of the organization, and if managers were smart enough to read the cards, what was disloyal about any employee, including those in the room, who looked for a job outside the organization? In fact, wouldn't it be in the best interests of both the organization and the employees, if every employee was given a regular opportunity to look at other options, with the help of outside job placement professionals and with no guilt attached?

It was clear that a raw nerve had been plucked and a norm had been challenged. Almost all the top managers had come up through the ranks. Those who were rising had never admitted even thinking about leaving. If done at all, it was done in secret, for fear of invoking the organization's anger. As happens in all cases where a value is questioned, the managers dug in their heels and initially rejected these ideas. In fact, they were angry at the consultant for raising the ideas! This example illustrates three barriers that organizations must deal with as they shift to the new paradigm.

- It is a deep-seated value in many old-paradigm organizations that leaving the organization—or even thinking of leaving or engaging in exploratory interviews—is a sign of disloyalty. In these organizations, employees test the external employment market in a climate of secrecy and organizationally engendered guilt.

- Organizations carrying this value into the new paradigm are unnecessarily burdened and restricted. Helping and encouraging employees of all levels to leave, whether or not they are on the high-potential list, is often the best strategy for both the organization and the individual. The individual gains revitalization and a sense of responsibility; the organization creates mobility, gains flexibility, and reduces costs.

- Managers operating in the crosscurrents of a paradigm shift have difficult and painful jobs. They must often discard values and belief systems that made sense to them on their way up the organizational career ladder. This act requires great personal courage.

Two basic tenets of the old employment contract for the individual were, I am grateful for my job, and I will plan a career within the organization. The two reciprocal organizational strategies were, we will take care of our employees, and we will only promote from within. The new employment contract realities are: organizations cannot keep their end of the bargain and thus create mistrust, and the result of promoting from a limited and internally conditioned labor pool is a narrow work force that is not responsive to the new paradigm. The new paradigm demands the Level 4 intervention strategies of legitimizing in/out career paths and recruiting for employee diversity.

Legitimize In/Out Career Paths

It is unrealistic for an organization to expect a lifetime commitment from an employee. It is not healthy for employees to collude with organizations in creating this counterfeit expectation. In the new paradigm, employees should be encouraged to move in and out of organizations as their and the organizations' needs dictate. When they are out, they can gain experience from related employment in other organizations, further their education, try something completely new, or consult. When they are in, they can focus on a specific, time-bound assignment where they are task oriented and able to do self-fulfilling work. When they are out, they can become revitalized. When they are in, they can focus on good work. Of course, transitions in or out of organizations may be painful, take time, and involve uncomfortable changes. They often require struggle at the financial, interpersonal, and organizational levels. Such transitions are, however, necessary and constitute a major activity in the new paradigm. There are at least three actions organizations can take to facilitate in/out career paths.

- *Eliminate penalties for returning.* Despite all the evidence that a new paradigm is operating, a number of organizations still will not rehire employees who leave on their own. Organizations that do rehire often penalize employees by making them restart benefit waiting periods or vacation accrual. It is vital that organizations stimulate rather than discourage in/out career paths. Benefits and other support services should not discriminate between those who stay and those who leave and return; these services should simply be available to help support all employees.

- *Develop processes to stimulate leaving.* Organizations should consider a mandatory career review at fixed time increments — for example, every three years. This is not a normal performance appraisal. Rather, it is a time when employees can review their life and career options in a safe, objective manner. Career reviews work best if outside experts such as financial advisors and outplacement specialists assist employees during the reviews. The result of a review may be a decision to "reenlist" in the same job, to explore different options internally, or to leave the organization, either in the short term or at a planned future date. Regardless of the decision, it should be guilt free for the employee and sanctioned by the organization. Although processes using outside experts can be expensive, their cost needs to be weighed against that of keeping a nonproductive employee or, worse, that of future layoffs.

- *Tell the truth up front.* Employees should be told the truth from day one, beginning with the initial employment interview and again during the new-employee orientation process. The truth is that the organization cannot guarantee that, if employees do a good job, they can count on a job until they retire or choose to leave. New employees can be offered opportunities for learning, performing good, challenging work, and working in a safe, clean environment. Any opportunities beyond that are conjectural in the new employment contract. Other truths employees should hear are that employees need to set boundaries, establish a diffuse root system, and to establish a nondependent relationship with the organization.

Many organizations resist suggestions that they tell the truth up front, because they assume it will be counterproductive. "You want me to tell them *that* the first day?" shouted an otherwise enlightened top manager. "How will they ever stay motivated?" But the organization did tell employees "that," and they not only stayed motivated, they appreciated the honesty. True motivation comes from investment in a task and the joy of good work, not from colluding in the old-paradigm concept of loyalty that both the employee and the organization, deep down, know is false and irrelevant.

Accelerate Diversity Recruiting During Tough Times

Employee diversity is the fuel of the new-paradigm organization. The external market is diverse, fragmented, global, situational, competitive, and demanding of service and quality. The internal skills to handle and relate to this new market rely on diverse perspectives, new ideas, and fresh approaches.

Successful new organizations will have a continual inflow of people of diverse work experience, gender, age, ethnicity, and data-gathering and decision-making style who will create the organization's competitive edge. The only way to acquire and maintain this needed competitive edge is through external recruiting. Old-paradigm organizations that only promote internally have an increasingly narrow pool of very similar people from which to select. The diversity grows ever narrower as one moves toward the top of the pyramid. The reason members of top management teams are often perceived as all looking the same is that they often are the same. In many old-paradigm organizations, they not only look the same in terms of age, gender, race, and dress, but through culturally conditioned inbreeding they often think alike, gathering data and making decisions similarly. In the new paradigm such homogeneity is the harbinger of a going-out-of-business curve.

When societies are relatively stable, as U.S. society was in the post–World-War-II era, organizations can get by with the inherent arrogance of a homogeneous perspective. In today's less predictable times, organizations need new voices and heterogenous perspectives. It is very difficult to bring new and different people into organizational systems that are in trouble. It is even more difficult to empower them and listen to them. It is, however, vital that organizations make this effort.

FROM AN IMPLICIT
CAREER COVENANT TO
AN EXPLICIT JOB CONTRACT

The play *How to Succeed in Business Without Really Trying* (1962), set at the height of the old paradigm, was based on the premise that the hero would "play it the company way," and whatever the company told him, that was "okay." That is really the way it was in the old days. The employee would behave in accordance with the culture, and the organization would offer him, or less often her, a permanent career. It was a long-term win-win relationship, and it enabled the employee to make long-term personal plans (financing a mortgage, serving in the local community, and keeping children in the same school system), while the organization could count on a stable, manageable, culturally conditioned labor force. The common denominator for these plans was continued organizational growth and global competitive dominance. Unfortunately, the growth resulted in bloated organizations, many of whom found their lunch being eaten by a foreign competition that was more responsive to customers' changing needs. The result was a painful dissolution of the old understanding between employees and business organizations, with not much to take its place.

What is beginning to emerge now is a new shorter-term and more specific employment contract. The relationship is still win-win, but it is more equal. The employee does not blindly trust the organization with his or her career. The organization does not assume an unassumable burden. The tremendous energy once required to maintain relationships can be turned to doing good work. The common ground, the meeting point, is not the relationship, but the explicit task. This task-focused relationship is not only healthier for the individual and the organization, it also facilitates the diversity necessary for future survival, since the emphasis is on the task, not on the gender, race, or traits of the person performing the task. The new employment relationship is much more explicit than the old and may involve specific formal contracts for tasks.

Despite its benefits, the new employment relationship is often confusing and frightening to organizations and employees alike. It goes far beyond the current standard relationship with temporary or contract employees (whose ranks are ever increasing as the new paradigm unfolds). To help readers understand the concerns of managers facing Level 4 interventions, this chapter ends with excerpts from recorded from a brainstorming session in which five executives addressed the employee-contracting concept.

MANAGERS' REACTIONS TO EMPLOYEE CONTRACTING

Our task is to talk about what we think are advantages to establishing a contractual relationship with all employees, regardless of level or tenure in the company would be. The rules of brainstorming apply — no evaluation, just ideas.

Employee Contracting Advantages

- It would clearly be a way of differentiating pay for performance. If you would have specific parameters for time and cost and task, you would have pay for performance much more clearly linked [to outcome] than we have today.

- It would require increased responsibility on the part of the employee in the relationship with the organization.

- Since expectations would be clearer up front, there would be fewer surprises and feelings of disappointment and betrayal.

- There would be greater emphasis on power of the professional contribution as opposed to power of position based on titles, office, other supporting things.

- It would respond to the needs of the individual in terms of career change and career flexibility. We would be similar, by way of model, to what the sports industry is doing, what the acting industry is doing, what the academic community is doing.

- It fits with the just-in-time employment concept, so that the organization will have the right number and types of people for the duration it needs and can quickly change that when necessary.

- It could make the task of human resource planning possible with a shorter turnaround time and responsiveness to acquiring the kinds of people you need.

- It would force our very senior managers to be much more strategic and much less transactional and remote, because their job wold be to manage a whole series of interlocking contractual relationships around implementing a strategy to which they agree.

- It would eliminate not knowing from one day to the next whether you have job security. You have a limited amount of security for a defined period time. Security could be extended more than year to year because the contract could be self-renewing.

- [As there is in] marriage, there is a desire for continued active commitment and recommitment and not taking the relationship for granted, so that both employee and employer see this as a partnership in terms of continuing to be a viable business entity, rathe than assuming everything will be taken care of.

Employee Contracting Disadvantages

- [It would be a] complex administrative process. . . . an administrative nightmare.

- [It would require] a great shift in thinking and expertise on the part of both employees and managers.

- It would require a great deal of change in attitude for those who are uncomfortable with anything new and innovative.

- It goes against the need for connectedness and affiliation.

- It treats people like things and will probably get people to act like things — *commodities* is a better term.

- If the economy goes bad in society as a whole, rather than organization's sharing responsibility for the welfare of [society's] citizens, it would be an everybody-for-themselves environment.

- In some way [success] would depend on other parts of business and industry [doing] similar things, in order to accommodate the coming and going of professionals.

- [It prevents] the advantage of having a built-in core labor force that is loyal to the organization, that can be counted upon.

- [It] would encourage the mentality of portfolio management vis-à-vis employees. Bring 'em in, kick 'em out, whenever necessary.

- We could end up without the necessary talent if everybody didn't renew their contract.

What Contracting Would Look Like: Some Scenarios

- If you had a typical office — let's say fifteen secretaries, two middle managers, sales managers, and a general manager — my vision is that the secretaries would have a relatively standard contract that renewed itself every year, that spelled out terms and conditions of employment, their attendance, their severance pay if they leave. The next level, the supervisor, might have a two-year contract that doesn't automatically renew itself, with some clear performance standards relative to productivity indexes. The senior person would have possibly a four-year contract with termination provisions in the middle of it and with very clear financial goals. If [the senior person] didn't meet those, the contract would not renew itself. The sales managers would have different goals, almost like our current sales incentive plan.

- I see what you're saying. For example, let's say that the organization wants a management development system. It would define if it means all managers going through certain prescribed training courses despite where they work. If that's my initial mission, then someone gives me a contract to do that, it would certainly make my job much easier and their job much easier because they've already contracted, they've paid me to do it so you wouldn't get a lot of "What was that objective again?" It would be much more clear going in, in terms of the outcomes. I would say, "Fine, I'll give you a system. It will take three years. I need ten people and I need three million dollars, and I need to have a facility. Here are the benchmarks. . . . At the end of those three years, here's what we'll get."

- There's difficulty there, if you make the contracting relationship so hard that it goes beyond one-on-one, with our current management process, you've got to get zillions of people to agree on something.

- It certainly does put a priority on the planning function. Let's say that you contract with a person to build you an executive succession planning system. The first thing you have to have is a clear shared vision of what the completed executive succession planning system process looks like, which forces communication. Second, you have to have some benchmarks of what it's going to look like in

January and March and June, so that you can check it. You wouldn't just want to wait for the two-year period and have it not happen. So it really does put a premium on shared goal setting and on benchmarking.

- The thought would be the same as when we go out and hire headhunters. Half the time the headhunter coming in is saying, "Okay, you've got to pay me anyway. What are you looking for again? And why do you want to hire this person outside? And what are the specs? You've got to pay this much money to get that person." We'd say, "We don't want that." What happens is, by going through the contracting process, you end up having a lot clearer values. The same thing [is true in] the example. If someone wants to hire someone to build us an executive succession planning system, [the person hired would say,] "It's going to cost us $1 million, it will take two years, here's what it's going to look like — okay?" It would force the company to really think through its commitment before launching. Something else it would do is take all the garbage and junk out that you end up getting involved in. Things would be clearer.

- One flaw to all that is the rest of the world is not in tune with it. Take the manager in his mid-fifties. He says, "Where do I go now?" And there's no support system to help him out of that nest he's now in.

- Part of what I'm thinking as we talk about this is that we're getting down into a whole lot of unrealistic stuff and that stretches our thinking. But, on the other side, I'm getting a greater sense of comfort that what we're talking about is an employment relationship that, in a more structured way, introduces these elements which probably should exist today, but do not. So that we're almost bringing in contractual terms and just using them in our current situation.

Employee Contracting Thoughts

- I'm encouraged because . . . it addresses aspects of issues that we are troubled by right now. Second, I think it has a plausibility. In fact, it only seems to require a shift in what we're already doing.

- It would cause people to rethink the work relationship. I think in the short term the headaches would outweigh any benefits to be gained from it, so I think there is a short-term cost. And short term is probably the first three to five years.

- We have to be sensitive to where people's heads are today. I think people's heads are in every bit as bad a spot as our survey data indicates. So I think we should do something. Clearly, plateauing and lack of commitment, all the things that we are talking about, are an issue to all organizations. I'm for explicit employee relationships. I'm for a more explicit relationship relative to development and renewal than we have today. So I think there is meat here.

- We are heading in a direction that is the next logical step in employment relationships within America. It is strategic in its responses to strategic issues. I think that it is exciting in the sense that it builds on existing tools, but with an important difference. Traditionally, we have focused our tools on the starting of jobs, on the starting of relationships—things that need to be done. We are now also adding to that to focus [up front] on the ending of jobs . . . through contingency.

ELEMENTS OF EXPLICIT CONTRACTUAL RELATIONSHIPS

Figure 10.1 illustrates a model of employee contracting. The model contains the seven elements that organizations should include in contracts with employees.

Figure 10.1. Contracting Model.
(Seven Components of a Contract)

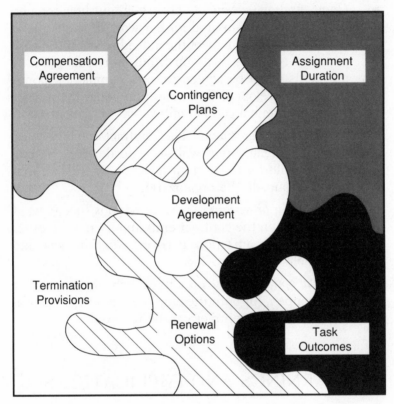

- *Task outcomes.* This is a clear, unambiguous statement of the work to be done, along with task benchmarks and key indicators.

- *Agreement duration.* This is the agreed-upon time for the task. If the task is a project, the time frame extends to the completion date. If the task requires an ongoing process, the time frame extends to the date the agreement expires and renewal does or does not take place.

- *Contingency plans.* These are the "what ifs." What if unanticipated changes take place at either the organization

or individual level? Contingency plans often lead to the
termination provisions.

- *Compensation agreement.* This spells out how the person is to be compensated for her work. It should be as
flexible as possible to meet the individual's needs. A cash
payment could be made up front, individual monthly
payments could be agreed to, or a completion bonus
could be developed. Compensation could be in cash,
stock, or in enhanced benefits.

- *Development agreement.* The contract spells out the
effort the organization will make to develop the employee's skills for the current task or new skills for jobs
inside or outside the organization.

- *Termination provisions.* These provisions specify what
happens when the contract ends and there is no other
work in the organization. It covers what financial and
other help will be provided.

- *Renewal options.* These options describe the results that
must happen, for both the employee and the organization, before the contract can be renewed.

LEARNINGS AND IMPLICATIONS

Level 4 interventions are the supporting and complementary
systems changes that will promote the climate that invites
individual empowerment and autonomy. These new-paradigm
systems changes can foster the individual acts of courage
necessary to break organizational codependency. Level 4 interventions are chicken and egg situations. It is hard to say
which comes first, the change in the system or the change
in the individual, because the two changes are totally inter-
dependent. Neither is easy or lends itself to a prescription
or a quick fix. Moreover, the need for change is no one's fault;
it is a systems issue. The implicit assumptions in the old em-

ployment contract fit the competitive and social environment of their time, but the same seeds that blossomed in the soil of the old reality sprout weeds in the new reality.

The mismatch that comes from old strategies played out in a new environment does not feel right from either the organizational or the individual perspective. Those who manage and lead organizations must make the same accommodations to the new reality as those in nonmanagement roles. In addition, top managers have the challenge of keeping the system together during a time of fundamental change. They need the skills, courage, and survival sense to take whatever risks are necessary to align organizational systems with the new reality and wrest control away from a paradigm in its death throes. These skills are the subject of the next chapter.

Part Four

The Great

Wake-Up

Call

11

The Rebirth of Meaning
and Direction:
Leading the
New Organization

*"Tell us something that sounds like it's coming
from someone's heart and not from their ledger."*

In order to create and sustain
organizations that have structural immunity to layoff survivor
sickness, leaders must guide these organizations through the
messy reality of a paradigm shift. This requires a combination of personal growth and risk taking. As one frustrated manager said, "My job is where the rubber hits the road in all this
paradigm change crap!" Being responsible for major change
while experiencing it is not an assignment that many people
can take calmly. It is an emotional challenge as well as a leadership challenge.

CULTURE BUSTING

Letting go of the old employment contract is not easy. At a transition workshop, for example, an angry group of general managers who had caucused at the bar the night before came to a session ready to do battle. Our dialogue was short and pointed.

"We don't buy into a lot of that stuff," said the spokesperson. "It takes away all the tools we have to manage!"

I said, "Yes, it does."

"It isn't fair."

"No, it isn't."

"The new way may not work either."

"It might not."

"It busts up the culture we've spent so long creating."

"Culture busting hurts."

"You're damned right!"

I remember this little dialogue both because of its intensity and because it drove me to invent the term *culture busting*. It is a powerfully appropriate term for the new-paradigm leadership challenge. Culture busting *is* necessary! Culture busting *is* painful! It is all the more so for the leader who must destroy that which he or she created in the past, in order to make meaning for the future.

Cross-Paradigm Meaning Making

One of the interesting new ways the Center for Creative Leadership is beginning to think of leadership is that leaders are meaning makers; they structure a confusing and ambiguous environment toward some unifying purpose (Drath and Palus, 1993). This concept defines leadership in terms of process: any individual or group who can create a galvanizing meaning is exercising leadership, regardless of the individual's or group's formal organizational role. The basic task of new-paradigm leadership is making meaning. Although anyone can, and often does, exercise leadership in a new-paradigm organization, I define the true organizational leaders as those whose primary responsibility is to facilitate meaning and, within the meaning, direction. (As a result, I do not differentiate here between leaders and managers.)

Those who occupy meaning-making roles in the midst of a paradigm shift enter into an adventure in confusion, ambiguity, and risk. Although it is sometimes terrifying, it is also sometimes exhilarating, and it is always crucial to the survival of the organization. Not only is creating meaning out of the ambiguity accompanying the new employment contract an exceedingly complex and sometimes gut-wrenching job, it is also a job that is chronically undervalued. Even those who are doing it often depreciate the importance and difficulty of their role. Their self-doubts are fueled by outsiders. Nonpractitioners, including many behavioral scientists, have no experiential frame of reference with which to grasp the true level of stress and ambiguity facing leaders moving toward the new paradigm. These managers are envied, misunderstood, projected upon, stereotyped, categorized, and often dehumanized by those who study them. For these reasons, line managers find themselves face-to-face with the paradoxes of the new employment contract with little support. One helpful way for them to visualize their meaning-making role is that it facilitates movement from the comfortable old to the paradoxical and relevant new. This movement can be broken down into six specific shifts that the manager needs to bring about (Figure 11.1).

- *From motivational strategies that promote dependence to strategies that promote independence.* It takes courage and creativity to buck the tide of fifty years of successful practice and untether the ties of organizational codependency. Often the new-paradigm leader must go against both the tradition of the organization and the inclination of employees.

- *From the yearning for belonging to the necessity for autonomy.* In an age of transient relationships and increasing

Figure 11.1. Leadership Shifts Behavior
from the Comfortable Old to the Relevant New.

From		To
Motivational strategies that promote dependence	⟶	Strategies that promote independence
The yearning for belonging	⟶	The necessity of autonomy
The organization as a primary social system	⟶	Employment as an economic relationship
The leader as savior	⟶	The leader as helper
The desire for permanence	⟶	The reality of transience
The leader as purveyor of objective reality	⟶	The leader as a maker of meaning

interpersonal alienation, people often look to organizations to satisfy their affiliation needs, but organizations' ability to do so is limited.

- *From the organization as an employee's primary social system, to employment as an economic relationship.* The new employment contract is economic, not social, in nature. The employee engages in short-term good work, and the organization provides monetary compensation. It is impossible to interact within an organizational system, even over a short period, and not become part of a social system; forming relationships is essential to the human experience. However, new-paradigm leaders know there is a real hazard in investing too much social currency in the organizational vault.

- *From the leader as savior to the leader as helper.* Many employees have a propensity to deify leaders, particularly the top manager. The boss knows all the answers. Got a problem? Need something resolved? Get to top management and they will write a prescription for you! These are the unrealistic expectations that lead to layoff-survivor blaming behavior. Organizational leaders are often linked both hierarchically and laterally in chains of powerless codependency. The boss cannot solve the economic, social, and organizational factors that led to the new employment contract. The boss can put himself or herself in a helping relationship with employees. Initially, however, this often goes against the grain of both employee expectations and the temptation to the leader to play the savior.

- *From the desire for permanence to the reality of transience.* The new employment contract is short term for *all* employees. The organizational leader must first deal with his or her own temporary status, then have the courage to work counter to culturally derived expectations in order to help employees understand the new contract's transitory nature.

- *From the leader as a purveyor of objective reality to the leader as a maker of meaning.* Leaders are not only expected to have all the answers; the answers are expected to be logical, rational, and "objective." The great wake-up call for the new MBA is that real-world decisions are not made behind desks using analytical models or rational processes; they are made in hallways or on elevators and are based on incomplete, fragmented, and conflicting data. New-paradigm managers must deal with the dissolution of the old without any certainty of the new, yet they must also help others make sense out of change. This is their crucial task, and it is not a "soft" one. Larry Porter captures the grit needed when he writes, "It takes courage and creativity to move into a situation and make something positive out of it. There is sure to be at least one hidden agenda in every pocket. People expect us to make them feel better, or they hurt and they want us to accept their diagnosis and give them the prescription they have decided on, or they want us to eliminate all the symptoms. We may be the only person able to take a risk, to confront, to ask the fools hard questions" (Porter, 1978, p. 3).

Creating Internal "Market" Economies

There is a parallel, both in process and substance, between the culture busting within organizations and the dissolution of the Soviet Union and the realignment of its former republics. In terms of process, both transitions require courage and faith to move into the future with skills and perspectives honed in a past that may no longer be relevant. In terms of substance, both transitions are about the creation of market economies. In the former Soviet Union, free markets are forming. Goods and services are beginning to be sold and valued in the light of market demand. The transition, although ultimately empowering and efficient, is filled with frustration, trauma, anxiety, and pain. In organizations implementing the new employment contract, market economies are also evolving. Individuals are moving toward an economic as opposed to a dependency relationship with their organizations. Just as in Russia and Eastern Europe, as the old system unravels, a new one does not automatically and flawlessly take its place. The stress and pressure on leaders is enormous. People in both systems are experiencing the necessary pain of culture busting.

THE JAPANESE PARADOX

"Why is it," asked a manager, "that the Japanese are eating our lunch in the global market, yet they seem to be up to their necks in the old employment contract? They don't have to go through all these leadership changes. What do they know that we don't?" His question revealed what I call the Japanese paradox. As it is unfolding in the West, the new employment contract is temporary, task focused, and based on empowered individuals contracting for good work with one or more organizations. In Japan, the contract is long term, relationship based, and grounded in total organizational dependency. The Japanese organizations that have this long-term contract have helped to create competitive conditions that led to the recent heavy U.S. layoffs in the first place. Yet our response has been to create organizational cultures exactly the opposite of the Japanese ones. What is going on?

Cultural Fit

Japanese society as a whole has a culture that values conformity, teamwork, fitting in, and subordination of the individual to the system. The United States has a cultural heritage of rugged individualism, of exalting the person over the system. In a sense, the old employment contract was a graft of collectivism on an individual-based culture, a mismatch in itself and one that may account for an underlying current of individual alienation from and dissatisfaction with organizational systems during the past fifty years. In Japan, the fit between national and organizational cultures is natural! What becomes unhealthy organizational codependency in an individual-centered culture may be the normal order of things in what Geert Hofstede (1980) calls a *high context culture*.

Artificial Homogeneity

The times they are a-changin', and there are those who see the golden age of an overarching Japanese homogeneity in decline. Japan has yet to replicate the U.S. experience of ferment and a seething, deeply felt debate over the implications of plurality and such manifestations of diversity as ethnicity, gender, age, disability, values, and sexual orientation. But there are signs that Japan may also experience this debate. Young Japanese professionals, particularly those who have worked overseas, are questioning the spirit-numbing work ethic. Women and ethnic minorities are nibbling at the edge of the Japanese all-male business aristocracy. If diversity is a competitive advantage, Japan has yet to pay its dues. The paradox within the paradox is that, although Japan competes in a diverse, multicultural, global environment virtually sizzling with change, its own system is fixed, monocultural, and based on feudal principals of filial obligations. U.S. organizations are emerging from their cultural struggle and entering the new paradigm, while Japanese organizations may just be entering their own struggle. If Japan's struggle results in a competitive disadvantage and subsequent layoffs, the manifestation of layoff survivor sickness in their culture of employee-employer loyalty will make what has happened in the United States look like a summer cold by comparison.

Short-Term/Long-Term Orientation

The United States increasingly operates within a system that demands instant results. In times of mergers, acquisitions, and speculation, only quarter-to-quarter profits count. Strategies that may result in short-term losses in order to develop long-term markets are not easily tolerated by the U.S. system. Japan, on the other hand, does take a long-term approach.

The U.S. government looks upon collaboration and cooperative market segmentation as restraint of trade. The Japanese government sees it as a way to develop global markets.

In Japan, the acquisition of new professional employees is seen as one of the most important activities of a firm. These employees are long-term assets to be nurtured over time. They are recruited very young, developed throughout their careers, and retired relatively early. What in the United States is age discrimination, in Japan is human resource planning.

The logical extension of a short-term orientation is the new employment contract. The outgrowth of Japan's orientation and culture is a version of the old employment contract.

Future Synthesis

Following Hegel's system of thesis and antithesis leading to synthesis, one can predict an eventual coming together of the two systems. Within the framework of the new employment contract, U.S. organizations are using total quality approaches, and self-directed work groups are emerging to pursue team-based good work. In Japan, organizations are beginning to explore the long-term competitive advantages of plurality and issues of work-leisure balance.

LEADERSHIP COMPETENCIES WITHIN THE NEW PARADIGM

Although the new paradigm is a strange and confusing place, many of the more analytical managerial skills can be transported from the old paradigm and used to illuminate dark corners of this new world. Some generic functional competencies such as marketing, financial planning, accounting, and strategy formulation can, with a tweak in time orientation, be carried over intact. Other dimensions of leadership require much more new skill development. These dimensions involve making transitions, creating visions, empowering employees, understanding oneself, exemplifying congruent values, and understanding the significance of process.

Transition Facilitation Skills

Today's leaders must know how to accomplish individual and organizational transitions. This is a competency not taught in business schools or most executive development programs. It is not an abstract analytical process carried out in the sterile confines of the executive suite or the manager's office. It is a hands-on, dirty, sweaty, humanity-filled, emotionally laden, risky process! It puts the leader's skin in the game. It moves him or her from the role of detached observer and manipulator of the levels of power to full-fledged participant in the action. It is the most important arena in which a new-paradigm leader can be relevant.

In addition to basic competencies in helping skills, today's leaders need conceptual models of the transition process. Jerry Harvey has often said that one of the best organizational interventions is a good book. Similarly, I have found that one of the best gifts I can give to a client is a conceptual model.

Models serve both as a frame of reference and as a way to get everyone speaking the same language and to secure understanding and commitment.

Effective leaders do not have to be academic organizational theorists. It is, however, important that they have a clear model for making transitions. No one model is best, but the one selected should be shared, so that the organization can create collective meaning. Of the myraid transition models available, I have found the following four to be of most use to working leaders in real organizations.

- *Bridges's transition model.* Perhaps the model that organizations find most useful when struggling through both organizational and personal transitions is that outlined by William Bridges (1980, 1988). Bridges postulates a stage theory (events take place in a predictable sequence) in which the first event is an ending. This ending is followed by a "neutral zone," which in turn is followed by a beginning. What new-paradigm leaders find most interesting in Bridges's model is the neutral zone. It is a time of floundering, a necessary period of ambiguity before a new beginning can be effective. If leaders rush the process, moving directly from an ending to a beginning without an intervening neutral zone, a true transition does not take place. Most layoffs move from reductions on a Friday to anticipated productivity gains the following Monday. One reason these gains do not take place is that survivors do not have the necessary neutral zone time and thus never make a true ending. Rebound marriages that do not last and post-layoff job changes that leave survivors alienated and unfulfilled are examples of the ways people rush the transition process without having the patience to pass through the neutral zone. In survivor workshops, I often pass out copies of Bridges's first book (an easy "read" and available in paperback) and then design exercises around it. I highly recommend it for leaders experiencing personal or organizational transitions.

- *Lewin's unfreezing, moving, and refreezing model.* This is a classic and very straightforward transition stage theory that has a great deal of appeal to managers (Marrow, 1969). A triggering event, or a wake-up call—such as layoffs—causes the system to see things differently. It "unfreezes" the system. Once the system is unfrozen, it can be changed, moved in a different direction, and taught to perceive reality differently. Systems, however, demand some consistency and thus need to be "refrozen" after the change is in place. Individuals move through transitions in the same stages. The old employment contract's failure, layoff survivor sickness, and global competition are triggering events for employer and employee unfreezing. Their movement is the implementation of the new employment contract. Their refreezing establishes the new employment contract as a system. This is a useful model for managers because of its macro and micro versatility. Most organizations continually experience a limited number of macro (longer-term) and a larger number of micro (shorter-term) unfreezes, moves, and refreezes. This old proven model's simplicity and versatility fit well into the new-paradigm leader's volatile world.

- *Individual crisis and stress models.* Leaders find it useful to have transition models that legitimize their feelings. A shared model also makes it easier for them to disclose their feelings to others. In addition to the Kübler-Ross model (Chapter Eight), there are two other valuable stage theories about people's emotions during transitions. The first is that of the Levinson Institute's Ralph Hirschowitz (1974), who outlines a four-stage sequence: impact (when the event takes place), recoil-turmoil (when the emotional reaction occurs), adjustment (when accommodation begins), and reconstruction (when the person puts the pieces together again). The second, and related, model is that of Stephen Fink, Joel Beak, and Kenneth Taddeo (1971), who identify the same four stages but give them

different names: shock, defensive retreat, acknowledge-
ment, and adaption and change. Managers find these se-
quential stage theories with their clear straightforward
language very helpful for understanding their own survivor symptoms and for establishing a common language
with which they can communicate with others.

Visioning Skills

Leaders operating within the new paradigm need to stimulate the creation of a galvanizing vision—an idea that pulls
the organization together. At the same time, they must guard
against being seduced into the savior trap. The last thing organizations groping their way through the new reality need
is a grandiose vision that flatters top manager's egos, but has
no value to the organization. Organizations need handles, pic-
tures of the future that employees and leaders alike can hold
on to and move toward. At times, a vision may simply be the
process of "regrouping" (Marks, 1991a) after a layoff. Visions
are not restricted to the end states of major strategic change
efforts.

The creation of a vision is an act of collective meaning
making, not simply the act of a single leader. Visions are collectively, not individually owned. The visioning skills of top
organizational managers can be the ability to hear and align
the visions of others. In addition, it is a myth that visions must
always be rosy and totally positive for everyone. A key task
of new-paradigm leaders is to help employees move toward
something, but that something is not always immediately com-
forting. It could be the reality of short-term contractual employment with no long-term job security. An honest vision
is better than no vision or a phony "bright future" vision.

Value Congruence,
Empowerment, and Self-Understanding

Byrd (1987) discusses five leadership "skills": visioning, antici-
pating, value congruence, self-understanding, and empower-

ment. These skills are critical to relevant leadership within the new employment contract, yet three of them — value congruence, empowerment, and self-understanding — are not generally found in leadership literature or taught in business schools and executive development programs.

- *Value congruence.* Leaders need to walk their talk. In order to be effective in managing paradox and ambiguity, leaders must be visible and accessible to employees. They cannot say one thing and do another. The new world demands a personal helping relationship between leader and employee, not an abstract analytical or controlling relationship. There is no safe place for leaders who lack this skill. Their behavior must be congruent with their values or they will lose their personal integrity. A new-paradigm leader who has no personal integrity has no effectiveness.

- *Empowerment.* Organizational leaders either live by the E-word or die by its absence. The new employment contract requires empowered self-reliant employees bound together by good work. In order to lead, managers must facilitate this empowerment, receive it, feel it in themselves, and distribute it to others. I call this *three-hundred-and-sixty-degree empowerment.* Using situational skills the manager creates a full circle of empowerment with boss, peers, self, and subordinates. These skills involve coaching, "catching people doing things right," sharing power, creating shared and mutual visions, and valuing diversity. Each leader has an invisible quiver filled with an unlimited number of arrows that contain a variety of behaviors that engender empowerment. Leaders use every interaction to discharge an arrow to all those they work with. Leaders make meaning and distribute empowerment.

- *Self-understanding.* Leaders cannot be anything but in the way unless they are open to feedback and understand their impact on others. They must also be clear about their own needs, so that they do not knowingly or unknowingly work on their own agendas at the employees' or organization's expense. Leaders open the path to self-understanding when they let go of artificial, hierarchically imposed defense mechanisms and make themselves vulnerable to authentic communication and feedback.

Process Wisdom Skills

Peter Vaill (1984) writes of "process wisdom for the new age," meaning that leaders of tomorrow must distinguish means and ends, which often are tangled together. Knowing means from ends is equally important to an empowered work force. A process-wise leader can be both a participant in an interaction and an observer. A process-wise leader knows that no two situations are exactly alike, and he or she resists the temptation to deal in pat, prescriptive solutions. In order to understand and help employees, leaders need to experience them individually, personally, unfiltered by preconceived theories and abstractions. As much as leaders are tempted to experience others in the abstract, they must have the courage to interact with them in the moment. The new paradigm has many levels of reality and often presents irreconcilable paradoxes. The process-wise leader does not get hooked into a fruitless quest for the "one" answer.

DEVELOPING THE RIGHT STUFF

How do you acquire the skills, wisdom, and perspective necessary to perform a leadership role in the perplexing new world we are creating? How do you develop "the right stuff"? To paraphrase the response of a wizened professional writer (from whom I took a workshop years ago) to the question of how to become a relevant author: live a long time and live intensely. Seek a variety of experiences and remember them. Retain your sanity, and tell the truth!

There is much to be said for experience. An intriguing model is Plato's proposal for the development of philosopher-kings. After passing three successively more difficult examinations that would weed out all but a very few, the remainder of the candidates would be allowed to study philosophy. These candidates would be at least thirty years old and would spend five years in rigorous philosophical training. They would then return to society for fifteen years and earn a living with no special privileges. At age fifty, they would have the knowledge and experience necessary to assume a position of leadership. While this is not a workable way for us to train leaders, the combination of rigorous formal training and practical hands-on, mingle-with-the-masses experience does present a model. And as much as the Greeks needed philosopher-kings, our need for new-paradigm leaders is far more crucial!

Being a leader within the new paradigm requires taking unselfish responsibility for helping others wallow through continuing disequilibrium. In addition to the complex technical and functional competencies required of all general managers, there are three core relevancy skills for new-paradigm leaders: intrapersonal insight, interpersonal competence, and a commitment to continuous self-improvement.

Intrapersonal Insight

In order to be relevant to others and drive collective meaning making, leaders must understand themselves, yet many leaders do not have good insight into their effect on others, and some are not clear about their own values and motivations.

Leaders need ways to secure valid data about themselves and to explore behavioral options. One way leaders can start this process is to attend training programs that show leaders how to get small-group and instrumented feedback on their behavior. Of particular importance is three-hundred-and-sixty-degree feedback, which allows leaders to compare their self-perceptions with those of their boss, peers, and employees. A related feedback experience involves intense work within small groups whose members learn from their own data and give and receive feedback with the objective of opening themselves up to a wider set of behavioral options. This type of training, which I call *self-insight training,* is also known as *sensitivity* training or *T-groups.* (The "T" stands for "training.") T-groups carry a lot of baggage — most as a defensive carryover of old-paradigm values. Some is warranted. In the hands of nonprofessional trainers more harm than good has been done. The two ingredients that make this training live up to its potential are competent and healthy trainers, who want to help the participants achieve insight and not to grind trainers' own counterdependency axes, and healthy participants who are there to learn from their own data, and are not seeking, or in need of, a group therapy experience. A criticism of T-groups has been that the personal growth and insight experienced in the group could not be transferred to the workplace. This was true in the old paradigm because the concepts of the leadership job did not allow for much self-understanding. However, self-understanding and personal growth are key new-paradigm leadership competencies. Through these competencies, leaders learn about themselves so that they can perform their primary function of helping others.

Although organizational leaders are not therapists, much of what they do involves placing themselves in this helping relationship. They must do whatever is necessary to achieve and maintain valid data on themselves. Wise new-paradigm leaders create such internal systems as upward performance appraisals, sensing groups, opinion surveys, and instrumented feedback to stimulate a flow of valid data. Personal feedback is not usually easy to hear, and it often shatters the mental scripts that leaders write about themselves and attempt to act out, but wise and effective new-paradigm leaders accept the discomfort of burst bubbles as the price of relevance. Some organizational leaders have individuals who act as their reality checkers and designated feedback givers. This is a powerful and useful role for a good human resource person who does not let the need for approval or a rules administration orientation get in the way of saying what the boss needs to hear. However, this role can be also played by other people in the organizations. I call these people "Petes," after an archetypal character I met in one organization.

Pete's title was vice president, special projects. Although he reported to the organization's top person and had a lot of influence in the top management group, I couldn't figure out exactly what he did until the first day of a team-building session when the boss opposed a clearly necessary change. His ego was so deeply invested in the current system that the harder the top management group pushed for change, the deeper he dug in his heels. In fact, he grew so irritated that the meeting ended early and he and Pete went off to dinner by themselves. The next morning the boss opened the session by telling the group he had thought it over and was wrong—the change should take place! This was an amazing turnaround, given his strong resistance the day before. When I asked one of the other participants about it, he just smiled and said, "Pete got to him."

Later it became clear that "getting to" the boss was Pete's only real function. Pete and his boss, the general manager, had once been contenders for the top job in the organization. At the time, they were both about three years from retirement and were in their next-to-last jobs within that organization. When Pete was not selected, the arrangement they made was that Pete could remain in the executive suite, keeping his office and perquisites. All he had to do until he retired was to keep his ear to the ground and "tell the general manager the unfiltered truth." Pete was a personal truth teller, reality checker, and feedback giver to the top person. The boss didn't always agree with Pete's perceptions, but he took the time to hear them.

The arrangement worked because Pete was respected by the general manager and the rest of the organization, had no personal axe to grind, and did not manipulate the situation to increase his power and prestige. Not too many organizations can afford full-time Petes, or could find a person with the right balance of truth telling and humility even if they could afford a full-time Pete, but effective new-paradigm leaders find ways to hear the truth, or at least another's perception of the truth. There are lots of part-time Petes out there, and even a few more full-timers.

Interpersonal Competence

Chris Argyris (1973) popularized the term *interpersonal competence* in his classic work on intervention theory. Today's leaders must be interpersonally competent in order to establish authentic employee relationships, facilitate meaning, and provide direction. The basic helping skills that make up interpersonal competence include the ability to give and receive feedback in ways that are constructive and nondefensive, empathetic listening skills, the ability to reflect feelings, and the ability to be confrontive in a caring and nonjudgmental way. These are Helping Skills 101, the basic communication and counseling skills that allow clarity and facilitate straight talk.

Top organizational leaders are often undertrained in these basic skills, but in the new paradigm, not having these competencies is akin to not possessing basic reading or math skills; leaders are simply unable to function effectively without them. There are several reasons why old-paradigm organizational leaders fail to be interpersonally competent.

- A *macho, controlling culture.* In the old paradigm, "real" men do not reflect feelings, deal in empathetic dialogue, or ask for feedback. They make decisions, analyze, and control. Similarly, in the old paradigm women, who are culturally sanctioned to use helping skills, are undervalued. Yet helping skills have always been of great effectiveness in organizations.

- A *left-brain bias.* The right side of the brain controls our emotional and intuitive selves. The left brain is involved in analytical, rational thought. In the United States and other Western cultures, organizations have a left-brain bias that results in an overemphasis on formal logic, analysis, and rationality. The new paradigm has more balance, but in most organizations, even today, helping skills are much less valued than controlling and analyzing skills.

- *The myth of scientific management.* This is not scientific management as defined by Frederick Taylor (people can be taught to work systematically and can be factored into the production equation as machines). Rather, it has to do with the inferiority complex felt by business schools and management training institutions in relation to scientists and their subsequent overreaction as they tried to be scientific. There was, and unfortunately still is in many institutions, the idea that you can study humans the same way you study rocks. Anything that was intuitive, feeling, or smacked of our unique human spirit was driven out of business education for fear that it would not be good science. Thus, entire generations of leaders grew up under the false assumption that there was an objective management science.

- A *fear of softness.* At the zenith of the old paradigm there was a reaction to anything that was deemed "soft." This included feelings, relationships, empathy, and anything that was "touchy, feely." If you think about it, this is a strange norm, because being alive and human involves relationships, feelings, and connecting with others. However, the value was facts and figures—"hard" stuff! Even though such rock-ribbed disciplines as physics now report that facts are relative, the bias continues. Organizations still talk about human resources and training as the "soft" side of management. But not only are people issues as real as financial and production figures, they require just as much skill and strength. In addition, they require authenticity and the risk of self-disclosure. This is much more difficult than hiding behind a memo or stack of figures! The good news is that, despite all the reasons that organizations discount "soft" helping skills, there is a slow but steady revision in progress. Organizational leaders are finding that interpersonal competence is in high demand in the new paradigm, and as they make this discovery, they are not only picking up useful skills, they are realizing a new sense of personal relevance as they discover new behavioral options and plumb the depths of their own repressed capabilities.

- *The challenge of continuous self-improvement.* The primary meaning-making tool is the authenticity and straight talk of the leader. All who truly want to lead in the organization of tomorrow need to go through whatever self-discovery is necessary to hone their own authenticity and candor and to be as relevant as possible in dealing with the change that surrounds them. Continuous self-improvement is not easy. It takes courage to keep looking in the mirror and to assess what one sees. Cross-paradigm leadership demands personal involvement and human interaction, and in the final analysis, the only tools that work here are each leader's own creativity, self-insight, and compassion.

LEARNINGS AND IMPLICATIONS

Organizations are the arena in which the new employment contract is played out. If leaders are to develop systems that possess structural immunity to layoff survivor sickness, they must learn to use the skills and competencies that will facilitate the transition from the certain and comfortable old to the relevant but uncertain and confusing new. Leaders must make meaning in a time of profound change. They must stimulate the necessary culture busting. They must master new or neglected competencies such as transition facilitation, visioning, value congruence, empowerment, self-understanding, and process wisdom. Leaders do not acquire these relevant skills in traditional management development programs or business schools; yet these skills are the most important capabilities leaders bring to the new paradigm.

No one has yet designed a core curriculum to teach leaders the functional skills necessary to manage a complex business and, in addition, teach leaders to be authentic, congruent, self-aware, process wise, other centered, and facilitative in the midst of major cultural change. As a precondition to acquiring these needed relevancy skills, leaders must have a strongly developed set of democratic values and possess the courage to understand their own needs and agendas. The arenas in which these skills are cultivated include intrapersonal understanding (self-awareness); interpersonal competence (helping and empathy); and a continuous self-improvement (honing one's own mind and feelings as the primary instruments of leadership).

The bell tolling for the death of the old paradigm can also be heard as a wake-up call. Leaders, as well as other stakeholders in the organizational system, have a unique opportunity to make a choice. The new employment contract has cleared the air. For the first time in many years, employees can choose to capture their autonomy and self-direction. The final chapter reviews this basic existential challenge.

12

Life After Downsizing: Revitalizing Ourselves and Our Organizations

"Well, if it goes, I've had a wonderful time.
They've paid for my daughter's education,
and the food in my mouth, and lots of things
over the years. I guess what they're talking
about now is they can't promise us life
security forever. No company can."

In the final analysis, layoff sur-
vivor sickness is a good news/bad news proposition. First the
good news. The past fifty years of "enlightened" managerial
practice have created codependency between organization
and employee. Organizations have been paternalistic; with
the best of intentions, they have established systems to hook
employees into the system by taking care of them. Employees
have been seduced and conditioned into letting themselves
be captured, often putting their self-esteem and sense of
relevance into the company vault. As we have seen, violations
of this dependence lead to anger, betrayal, and depression—

the joyless, nonproductive funk of layoff survivor sickness. The stronger the dependence, the deeper the sense of violation when the dependent person is cut loose. Since most organizations who are now cutting back worked hard and long to create a dependent work force, most layoff survivors suffer survivor symptoms. Layoff survivor sickness is a serious, pervasive, and underestimated problem. That is the bad news.

Now, the good news. The shock of violated dependency is a clear and compelling wake-up call, an alarm that, if heeded, could do more to stimulate a truly empowered and autonomous work force than all the X, Y, and Z theories, false starts, and hollow rhetoric of the past. Past efforts at empowerment, autonomy, and internal market economies have not worked, because they took place within the paternalistic cultural constraints of the old paradigm. It was like grafting a peach limb to an oak tree; it might grow, but the fruit would be stunted and puny.

The state of our business organizations is now analogous to the state of affairs in what used to be the Soviet Union. The pain and the shock of the breakup of the past paradigm are frightening, but without this wake-up call, the possibilities for unleashing repressed human potential could not be tested. *Possibility* is the key word, since in the case of both the former Soviet Union and the new-paradigm organizations, the jury is still out on the ultimate results of the changes that are occurring. If heeded, the wake-up call could result in empowered employees linked to facilitative organizations by good work: a formula for productivity and global competitive advantage. If unheeded, the alarm could result in futile attempts to turn back the clock, with a resultant repression of human spirit and organizational relevance and productivity.

FRAGILE CHOICES

The failure of paternalistic organizations and the pain of violated dependency are forcing us to confront individual and organizational choice. Individuals who have taken the risk of breaking the shackles of organizational codependency require a supportive environment, yet organizations seeking to be relevant to the harsh demands of the new paradigm must move against the grain of strong cultures of the past. The fragility of new-paradigm organizational initiatives is illustrated by a firm I will call Midwest Services.

Midwest Services

Whenever I think of Midwest, I am reminded of the teacher portrayed by Robin Williams in the movie *Dead Poets Society*. Operating within the constraints of a paternalistic (old-paradigm) private school system, this teacher transformed his students from codependent, information-regurgitating, test-passing robots to empowered, autonomous learners. He gave them a metaphor for paradigm breaking by making them stand on their desks to see a new view of old things. In the end, however, he was fired, replaced by a traditional carrier of old-paradigm values. Paternalistic, control-oriented, codependent values once again ruled the classroom. True learning (good work) and organizational productivity (turning out adventuresome, autonomous learners) were sacrificed on the altar of old-paradigm conformity.

Midwest Services was a wholly owned, theoretically independent subsidiary of a regional financial services organization. A small organization (less than fifty people), Midwest offered specialized computer and planning services to financial institutions. For years, it has operated in a backwater of benign neglect from the parent, but under the leadership of a new president, it developed a number of structural innovations. This small organization did a lot of things right; it had self-directed teams, a flattened structure, outcome-related incentive pay, and a near obsession with straight talk and quality. These new-paradigm interventions paid off; profits went up, and new clients came in. It was a great place to work. You could feel the spirit when you walked in the door! How-

ever, true to the "unfortunate but predictable fate of the majority" of high-performing subsystems, it was not long before
the parent organization moved in. The unit was too different, the systems too unusual, the straight talk too disrespect-
ful and politically incorrect.

The triggering event was a team incentive plan. The parent organization did not have team incentives and would not
approve them for the subsidiary. The "empowered" president
implemented one anyway and was soon history. His replacement, a longtime parent organization careerist, "regularized,"
as he said, the organization. It was amazing how quickly the
carefully crafted autonomy and good work–oriented culture
was replaced by a control-oriented culture and political relationships. In less than a year, the new culture had been driven
underground or out the door (some of the employees left or
were laid off). After two years, profits had declined to the point
that the external business of the subsidiary was dissolved and
the few services that the parent was purchasing were brought
in-house. Absurd and wasteful though they may seem, these
events are not unusual. The pull of the old culture is strong,
and empowered employees and customer service are all too
often sacrificed to old values, even though those values are not
relevant to the new reality. Organizational response to the
wake-up call of the new paradigm is, in all probability, a choice
of growth and relevance or of atrophy and eventual death. Reciprocal choices must be made by employees. They can elect
organizational codependency, which will almost certainly be
violated at some point, plunging them into layoff survivor sickness, or they can choose self-control and empowerment, which
will equip them to thrive in the new paradigm.

Ralph's Reevaluation

Ralph was a fast-track design engineer in an organization that
developed weapons systems for the federal government. Hired
off the campus, Ralph, through technical competence and
labor shortages, floated upward on the rising tide of fat govern-

ment contracts for the first ten years of his career. At the age of thirty-five, he was a middle manager with two children, whom he didn't see as often as he liked, a large mortgage for a house he only slept in, and a wife who, out of boredom, worked part-time as a paralegal. When the contracts stopped coming in and his organization began to "take out" people, Ralph's world began to unravel. Although he struggled to hold on, the layoffs eventually caught up with him, and he became a victim. He was unemployed for nearly six months before being rehired into his former organization in a non-management role at a substantial reduction in pay.

Today, three years after his rehire, Ralph's cash compensation is only slightly less than he made before. His psychic income, however, has increased tremendously. He is doing what he perceives as more interesting and relevant work and putting in fewer hours. He has achieved a balance in his work and his life, seeing his work as a vital part but by no means all of his life. He knows there is a good probability that he will lose his job again, but feels confident that he will be able to make whatever accommodations are necessary to adjust when that time comes.

Paradoxically, by "not playing the game," by approaching his job as an individual entrepreneur, and by "telling the truth," he is getting the best performance reviews of his life, and reports having to "fight" against getting promoted to a managerial role again.

During his forced unemployment, Ralph also clarified his values.

- *Set priorities.* The time away from work helped Ralph appreciate his need to spend more time with his family. He decided that the price he was paying in terms of hours and sheer physical fatigue for his managerial role was not worth what he had received from that role.

- *Renew vows.* Ralph and his wife had drifted apart. As his job consumed his time and energies, there was not enough of either left to invest in his marriage. He and his wife decided that their personal relationship had priority over any organizational relationship and that they would not allow any new job to get in the way again.

■ *Assess economic needs.* Ralph and his wife decided they did not need the big house and agreed that there was more to life than servicing a mortgage. Their objective was to get out of a large fixed payment, not to make a huge profit, and they sold the house quickly. They now live in a smaller but adequate house in the same school district. They also cut back on some nonessential expenses. Ralph's wife increased her outside work hours during his unemployment and proved to both of them that she too could bring in significant income, if necessary, to make ends meet. Ironically, even though Ralph is making less and working shorter hours, he is able to save more in his new situation.

Breaking organizational codependency wasn't easy for Ralph. He went through anger and depression. He and his wife sought financial and career counseling, and Ralph participated in a support group. Even though Ralph has learned from his wake-up call and has achieved a sense of balance in his work life, his future is not without risk. Just like the recovering alcoholic, Ralph must maintain his perspective every day and work hard on maintaining a nondependent work relationship. However, when compared to Charles, the layoff survivor described in Chapter One, Ralph is leading a much more relevant and productive life.

THE EXISTENTIAL ACT OF CHOOSING FREEDOM

The gift to us of the wake-up call is that it helps us frame our choices. Few of us will have had the opportunity to wrest our autonomy from our organizational affiliation during the height of the old paradigm; we were too much in the paradigm to see it. If not fat, dumb, and happy, we were at least woefully ignorant. Now, many layoff survivors are neither fat nor dumb nor happy. Nor can they claim ignorance. They do, however, have the opportunity to make a real choice, and that may be a once-in-a-lifetime gift. Breaking organizational codependency and taking responsibility for our own work is our ultimate existential challenge. We cannot abstract it, delegate it, or have a task force study it. We must do it and be it! It is a tenet of existential philosophy that as we move away from an artificial dependence we are moving toward our essential nature, which is freedom. Accepting this natural state of freedom after years of dependence is not easy. To the philosopher Jean-Paul Sartre, we are "condemned" to be free (Sahakian, 1971, p. 354).

Nevertheless, making the choice to immunize ourselves to layoff survivor sickness by breaking organizational codependency is an affirming act, something we do, not something we abstract. Peter Block (1987) frames it with action verbs when he writes of "choosing an entrepreneurial path" (p. 11), or "claiming our autonomy" (p. 101). We have the opportunity to make a choice. We do not have to be dragged back into old-paradigm codependency. Stephen Covey (1989, p. 310) captures the meaning of this opportunity when he celebrates the gap between stimulus and response: "I reflected upon it again and again, and it began to have a powerful effect on my paradigm of life. It was as if I had become an observer of my own participation. I began to stand in that gap and to look outside at the stimuli. I reveled in the inward sense of freedom to choose my response — even to become the stimulus, or at least to influence it — even to reverse it." We hear the death toll of the old paradigm as a wake-up call, and our response defines both our individual sense of relevance and autonomy and our organization's growth and survival. If we claim our independence and shed the manipulation and control of organizational codependency, we embark upon an existential voyage of discovery. We will never reach the end of this voyage; it is another tenet of existential philosophy that we are always in the process of becoming, and never being. But what a voyage it is, filled with self-esteem, relevance, and pride of contribution fueled by good work and unmarred by manipulation or futile attempts to control the uncontrollable!

LEARNINGS AND IMPLICATIONS

I have written both about layoff survivor sickness as the symptom and unhealthy dependence as the disease. The phenomena are interlinked, and we must work on both halves of the equation simultaneously. The depth and toxicity of layoff survivor sickness is not well understood, and is often denied. Thus, I devoted the first six chapters to deepening our understanding of the pathology and debilitating nature of survivor symptoms.

The last six chapters dealt with methods of intervention. I described a model with four levels—the first two dealing with symptomatic relief and the last two dealing with root causes—that organizational leaders can use in their own transitions from the old paradigm to the new.

We are living out the ancient Chinese curse; we *do* live in interesting times! We have the opportunity to turn pain into gain, to use the death toll of the old paradigm as a call for action, to give up our codependency and claim our autonomy and self-empowerment. Organizations have the opportunity to form structures and processes that shed the limitations of the old, control-oriented culture. The pay-off of empowered employees linked to facilitative organizations by good work is not just elimination of layoff survivor symptoms, it is individual relevance and global competitiveness.

Appendix A

The Survivor Groups

Ten groups of layoff survivors were chosen for study from a large client organization. These groups were based on diversity of employee level, type of business, and geographical location. Approximately 115 employees participated in these groups. Employees in all but one group had survived severe layoffs within the past year. Severe layoffs were defined as more than 5 percent of the work force within the past twelve months. A group interview instrument was developed that consisted of thirty-seven questions and problems. Eight to 15 employees participated in each group discussion. Each discussion was tape-recorded and lasted approximately two hours.

Eight of the interviews took place in various facilities in the client organization's headquarters. Another group met in the San Francisco area and another in a Washington, D.C., suburb. The eight headquarters-city groups were limited to single-job families: production workers, technicians/professionals, managers, executives, administrators and clerical employees. The group on the West Coast combined managers and internal consultants, while the East Coast group included technicians, sales people, and computer programmers (Table A.1).

The transcripts for all ten groups were analyzed for thematic frequency, in order to determine the major themes

Table A.1. Group Interview Demographics.

Location	Type of Organization	Group Number & Employee Type
HQ city	Design development and production	1. Technicians/professionals 2. Production workers
HQ city	Manufacturing	3. Production workers
HQ city	Engineering	4. Managers
HQ city	Federal contracts	5. Technicians/professionals
HQ city	Corporate staff facility	6. Executives 7. Administrators 8. Clerical employees
East Coast (field)	Sales office	9. Managers and consultants
West Coast (field)	Sales office	10. Technicians and salespeople

discussed within each group and to highlight any differences in concerns between employee levels. The interviews were conducted and content analysis performed by a professional external (nonemployee) research organization. Some themes were common to all groups while mention of other themes varied by group and type of employee (Table A.2).

Table A.2. Group Interview Themes.

Theme (What Group Members Felt)	Group
Insecure, uncertain, fearful	All groups
Depressed, tired, stressed	All groups
Perception of unfairness	All groups
Perception of reduced risk taking, lowered productivity	Executives, managers, field groups, technicians/professionals, administrators, clerical employees, production group 3
Frustrated, angry	Executives, managers, field groups, technicians/professionals, administrators, clerical employees, production group 2
Betrayed, distrustful	Field groups, technicians/professionals
Guilt	Executives, administrators, production group 3
Optimistic	Executives, managers

Appendix B

The Human Resource Study

Structured individual interviews took place with thirteen human resource professionals. This sample consisted of survivors from business units that had self-contained human resource functions. Participants were selected who had been heavily involved with layoff administration or had had face-to-face contacts, such as exit interviews, with employees in the process of being laid off. The interviews with the human resource professionals were taped, and the transcripts' content analyzed. The interviews were conducted and the analysis performed by professional (nonemployee) behavioral researchers. Percentages of descriptors used — words and feelings that, when analyzed, corresponded to general clusters of feelings — are shown in Tables B.1, B.2, B.3, and B.4.

PROJECTIONS OF SURVIVOR FEELINGS

Human resource professionals were asked to describe, or "project," the feelings of survivors. The three primary clusters of feelings attributed to survivors were insecurity; frustration, anger, and resentment; and expressions of positive morale (Table B.1). The typical comments of the professionals follow.

**Table B.1. Human Resource Professionals'
Descriptions of Survivor Feelings.**

Clusters of Feelings	Percentage of Descriptors
Insecurity (anxiety, fear)	34
Positive morale	21
Frustration, anger, and resentment	20
Stress	6
Depression	5
Confusion, loss of control	4
Other	10

Insecurity

"There is a nervousness there because [the survivors] know that they could potentially be impacted. There's a general uneasiness within the organization right now because of the feeling that something is going to happen."

"The greatest anxiety people experience is when they get rumors that there's a work force reduction coming up. There is no communication in advance of the rumors."

"They are still not totally settled, and so some of them are still looking over their shoulders and wondering, 'Am I next?' or 'What's going to happen next?'"

Frustration, Anger, and Resentment

"The greatest anger that I see is in the period of time from when the rumor or the first communication starts until things finally happen. People are under a great deal of stress through a long period of time. One organization has known since October that there are going to be changes. They have not been announced yet—that's six months."

"The January 20 work force reduction—the second wave—was very small, minute in number, compared to the damage it did. People thought we were done. They understood last year was bad. They understood we had budget problems. [The second wave, however,] just didn't make sense. And they're angry."

"I hear an awful lot of resentment over the fact that so much effort over the years has been given to projects that aren't presently being successful, and [the survivors] feel that their management has failed them."

Positive Morale

"Morale is pretty good. People really are bullish. . . . They are really wanting good things to happen here."

"We've still got a very loyal group of people who, come blazes or high water, they are going to be good troops. They'll carry our standard into battle anywhere."

"You come in here on a Saturday or Sunday and the parking lot over here is full. So you mean you have to re-recruit people who are working seven days a week? I don't think so."

Six of Nine Did Not Perceive Guilt

"I don't think [the survivors] feel guilty, because they feel they're doing their job and not that they're pointing the finger at somebody else. They feel that they're the worker bees, and the people that have made the decisions are the ones that got us into this."

"I think we see [guilt] during that period of time when people are on thirty-day notice, when you have to work alongside them. But for the most part, once those people are gone, once we get into the new structure or the new project or program, work continues."

DESCRIPTIONS OF SURVIVOR COPING STRATEGIES

When the human resource professionals were asked to project survivor coping strategies, they identified six ways the survivors coped with their feelings (Table B.2). Examples of their comments follow.

Table B.2. Human Resource
Professionals' Descriptions of Survivor Coping Behavior.

Coping Behaviors	Percentage of Descriptors
Reduce commitment to the job	23
Reduce productivity	20
Think business as usual	16
Work through the feelings	11
Develop contingency plans	9
Practice avoidance	7
Other	14

Productivity and Commitment

"Although [the survivors are] here and they're working, you know that they're doing the things that have to be done and they're not looking toward doing anything for the future."

"The most outstanding feelings that we've seen are, 'there is nothing I can do'—this helpless feeling, abandonment of any decision making or taking control of their own destiny. People just get tired of seeing [layoffs] over and over again, and they just kind of start putting in their time."

"Productivity has gone down significantly in general in the work group. But I don't think it's [because of] dealing with anger. I think it's basically the uncertainty of their jobs, . . . the rumor mill, the change in organization."

"When you really see the lack of productivity is during the uncertain period and as the cuts are happening. All that people do is sit around and talk."

"There isn't any productivity, at least where the known hits are going to take place. Everybody is standing around and behind closed doors, talking about what they think is going to happen. There isn't any productivity."

Short-Term Perspective

"[Layoffs tend] to shorten your perspective; you tend to plan on a shorter basis, tend to think more about longer-term purchases.

"A lot of people are riding it through for a period of time until they can find something else. The activity over the past three or four years caused their thinking to come down very short-term."

Need to Deal with Survivor Symptoms

"It's a mourning process you go through. We're beginning to recognize we have to help them go through it. We've made some efforts at communicating the manager's role in that process, but it's an uphill battle."

"There is more of a problem out there than meets the eye. We've got to take the lead. If we don't, who will?"

"We can make the numbers — that's not a problem. The real problem is an alienated labor force; that's the challenge for the next few years."

SELF-ASSESSMENT OF FEELINGS

The human resource professionals were asked to describe their own feelings. These descriptions were much more narrow and controlled than their descriptions of employees' feelings. They used approximately 50 percent more descriptors when talking about others than when discussing their own feelings. They tended to move from talking about themselves to employees in general or to their own staffs. They also reflected a different pattern of feelings than those they projected for other survivors, reporting more positive morale and less insecurity, frustration, and anger. The clusters of human resource managers' feelings are summarized in Table B.3, and sample remarks follow.

Positive Morale

"Interestingly enough, I and all of my group, many of whom have been through three to four years of [cutbacks, remained] relatively well in spirit. We had a lot of wins, a lot of highs;

Table B.3. Human Resource Professionals' Expressed Feelings.

Clusters of Feelings	Percentage of Descriptors
Positive morale	31
Stress	27
Depression	11
Frustration, resentment, anger	11
Insecurity	9
Other	11

we saw a lot of positives that came out of things that were happening for people. We placed a lot of people in other jobs."

"I go to a different city, and I work with people there, and I get really excited again. I start to believe that we could create a different kind of environment and that those plants there could survive if they would take charge as they are trying to. For me, that means I can put my energy into that."

"It's very stressful, but it is extremely rewarding. They want your input, and they are very appreciative of it."

"I still think we are a fine group of professional employees. The group I have has probably been never better as far as people are concerned."

"I've contributed so many years, and I'm willing to put more blood into the game."

Frustration, Anger, and Resentment

"There is very little support from my management. One day I did half a dozen exit interviews which were very difficult for me, and no one within my management chain has ever asked me how the interviews went."

"The experience had been shattering for me because of the ways that the company has treated people. It is a sin. As people left, the management team didn't say goodbye. It's like an admiral that jumped ship and, as he's leaving the sinking ship, tells people to keep it up as long as they can as the ship sinks. Management has told me to keep the people quiet and to get on with business."

"We need to take a hard look at executive management. . . . Many of our human resource executives have retired on the job and are holding strategic positions."

"You look out and say, 'Hey, wait a minute.' You have that function sitting there hardly doing anything, and it doesn't really appear to be at all necessary, and they're taking hours that could be turning the corporation around."

"I see conflict and unfairness over what the organization is giving to executives and to the rank and file. There was a situation in which they would not give an employee who recently had a child and bought a home an extra two weeks of work when there was work to do, and yet they have been giving very large termination packages to executives."

SELF-ASSESSMENT
OF COPING STRATEGIES

Human resource professionals were asked to assess their coping strategies. The coping mechanisms seemed related to the fact that the professionals possessed a greater amount of layoff information than the other employees and had greater involvement in the process. Table B.4 depicts the most frequently mentioned clusters of coping strategies. The human resource professionals spent a great deal of interview time justifying and providing explanations for the layoffs or their role in the layoffs.

Justifying

"But you also have to look at it from the business aspect. We're in a very competitive marketplace right now, and it's going to get more competitive. When you look at it from a standpoint that these are actions that we have to take in order to

Table B.4. Human Resource Professionals' Coping Strategies.

Clusters of Feelings	Percentage of Descriptors
Justifying, explaining	28
Openly expressing feelings working through emotional involvement	21
Distancing, denying	20
Experiencing productivity increases	11
Experiencing productivity declines	7
Developing contingency plans	5
Other	8

stay competitive and we're paying for a lot of sins of the past, there's absolutely no question that we're doing what has to be done to survive."

"Then your morale sinks, and I've gone through that. Then you reach the point of professionalism where you say [to yourself], 'Listen, you know you've got a job to do, you're carrying this burden, and you've got to do it and do it right, so get back to work.'"

"It's the worst part of a human resource manager's job, but it's a necessary thing that you have to face."

Distancing

"I can't personalize with them [the people being laid off]. It's just a matter of what's happening in the company. So why should I be down on myself or start feeling awful? It's not my fault anyway. I also believe that a lot of our employees feel that way."

"I have gotten to the point where I come and do my job every day, and I try to do it well. I have had to get to the point [where], when I got out of here, . . . I totally forget the people."

Productivity Increases

"We were committed to being here before the 8:00 A.M. start time. We would try and get our job done in the office, and then we would go to another facility, and we would spend six to eight hours or as many hours as we could there. Then at 5:00 P.M. or 4:30 P.M., we would go back to our normal office and try to get a lot of our job done. We felt we were really needed there. We dealt with it by getting the pats on the backs from the people and knowing that we were doing something that was needed. There was a level of energy that I hadn't seen before."

OTHER FINDINGS

The following remarks represent additional themes and areas of concern among the human resource administrators.

Need for Straight Talk

"We're not living in an environment of the past where there's been a lot of growth and hiring of people. We're going from a very stable environment to one of downsizing most of our job families."

"The strongest feeling I have is that the company is not going to make it if they continue to act the way they act, if the executives act the way they act. And in that I mean they don't face reality, don't face the truth of what's happening and continue to live in that ivory tower of, 'We're really good; we're really okay.'"

"Employees are really offended when the corporation tries to take something that is bad news and communicate it as good news. It is insulting to their intelligence, . . . and it makes them very suspicious of the next communication that comes out."

Profitability as a Cure

"What re-recruits people is not some program, some flashy program that somebody came up with, or some gimmick. It's a better business formula, a better profit picture, and with that will come the things that people need [if they are] to be re-recruited."

"It boils down to business. [The] remedy is to return to profitability and basically get us back on the right track, and maybe we can stop, stabilize the organization, get it down to where we have what I consider a core business . . . , and then go on and be successful. Then people will start feeling good again."

Need to Communicate Permanent Change

"Tell them where we're going, tell them what to expect, tell them what the new environment is."

"We need to communicate with people what the new company is going to be like so that their expectations change. Many are still expecting it's going to be as it was. If I change my level of expectation to a point where I can understand what the new system is going to be like, then I can make a decision whether I want to live with that or not."

INTERVIEWER RATINGS

At the conclusion of each interview, the human resource professional's intensity of layoff involvement; projection of the survivor of guilt, anger, and fear; and personal survivor feelings of guilt, anger, fear, and depression were rated. The results are summarized in Table B.5.

CONCLUSIONS
AND OBSERVATIONS

Individual interviews with human resource professionals who had been heavily involved with the layoff process represented a different set of lenses through which to examine both the survivor symptoms of the human resource professionals them-

Table B.5. Interviewer Ratings of Human Resource Professionals.
(*Number of Professionals*)

	Very Low	Low	Moderate	High	Very High
Intensity of layoff involvement	—	1	—	5	7
Projection of survivor feelings of:					
Guilt	1	7	5	—	—
Anger	1	2	7	2	1
Fear	—	2	5	5	1
Professionals' level of survivor:					
Guilt	1	11	1	—	—
Anger	—	8	2	2	1
Fear	1	8	2	1	1
Depression	1	8	1	2	1
Evaluation of subject's belief that there is a need to "re-recruit" the work force	1	1	3	5	3

selves, and their descriptions of the symptoms of their respective work forces. Although this was a small sample when compared to the group interviews (thirteen people, about the size of one of the ten groups), it represented a cross section of human resource manager survivors from a number of diverse business units.

Differences Between Survivor Descriptions and Self-Descriptions

The professionals' projected survivor feelings were similar to those reported in the group interviews by survivors themselves. Approximately 70 percent of the descriptors dealt with insecurity, frustration, anger, stress, depression, and confusion. These feelings dropped significantly when the human resource professionals described themselves. The cluster of insecurity, anxiety, and fear was most frequently projected for other survivors (34 percent of the descriptors). The most frequently appearing cluster for the human resource professionals was positive morale (31 percent of the descriptors). Human resource professionals also projected a much higher incidence of positive morale among other survivors (21 percent of descriptors) than the analysis of the group interviews indicates was the case. Although it is important to realize that survivor symptoms of stress, depression, anger, and insecurity existed in nearly 60 percent of the human resource professionals' self-descriptors, there is nonetheless a difference in the level and type of survivor symptoms projected for the employee population and those reported by the human resource professionals for themselves. This difference is reflected in self-descriptions of higher positive morale than in the survivor population at large, and lower self-reported levels of insecurity. This difference is also reflected in the interviewer's ratings (Table B.5).

The human resource professionals' perceptions of optimism are similar to those expressed by managers and executives in the group interviews. In both cases these perceptions may be related to the individuals' prior knowledge, participation in layoff decisions, and sense of control. The professionals' concentration on what they perceived as positive organizational outcomes may also have been a method for them to avoid dealing with their individual feelings. As I previously indicated, the human resource professionals tended to shift the focus of the interviews from themselves to others.

Similarity to Group Interview Results

The lack of reported survivor guilt, the presence of the layoff survivor blaming phenomenon, and the perceptions of a permanent change were all similar to the results of the group interviews in these areas.

Justification and Explanation

The human resource professionals spent a great deal of interview time explaining the economic needs for layoffs and justifying their individual roles. This was unique to the human resource interviews and did not emerge within the group interviews. One reason for this difference may be that human resource managers in the organization studied tended to act as a communication link between the management and nonmanagement population and had an organizational role of explaining the layoffs. Another reason may be that the explanations are that a form of the defense mechanism usually labeled as rationalization.

Since human resource professionals in this organization do, in a sense, live both in the world of the manager and that of the nonmanager, they often tend to be conflicted and concerned over their role. This may be a reason for the interview time spent in role discussion and the emergence of rationale that says, "It's a tough job, but someone's got to do it."

Alignment with Management

Although the human resource function in the organization studied is perceived by top management as having an advocacy role for employees, the results of the individual interviews indicate that, in the final analysis, these professionals align themselves with management. Their view is reflected both in their individual survivor descriptors and in their general concerns. They see management of the process of layoffs as important and relevant work, and they discussed it in a number of contexts. The values underlying layoffs, survivor feelings, and potential healing processes were discussed, but with less intensity and ownership.

Human Resource Professionals as Survivors

Although the perceptions of many of the human resource professionals differed from those of the general employee population, it is important to point out that these differences tended to be more in degree than in substance. Human resource professionals in the organization studied were still layoff survivors and had many more similarities with their fellow survivors than differences. They, along with the other survivors, exhibited both the survivor blaming phenomenon and a sense of permanent change. Stress, depression, anger, and insecurity constituted nearly 60 percent of the human resource professionals' feeling descriptors.

References

Argyris, C. *Intervention Theory and Method: A Behavioral Science View.* Reading, Mass.: Addison-Wesley, 1970.

Bardwick, J. M. *The Plateauing Trap: How to Avoid It in Your Career and in Your Life.* New York: AMACOM, 1986.

Beattie, M. *Codependent No More: How to Stop Controlling Others and Start Caring for Yourself.* San Francisco: Harper-Collins, 1987.

Block, P. *The Empowered Manager: Positive Political Skills at Work.* San Francisco: Jossey-Bass, 1987.

Bridges, W. *Transitions: Making Sense of Life's Changes.* Reading, Mass.: Addison-Wesley, 1980.

Bridges, W. *Surviving Corporate Transition: Rational Management in a World of Mergers, Layoffs, Start-Ups, Takeovers, Divestitures, Deregulations, and New Technologies.* New York: Doubleday, 1988.

Brockner, J. "Managing the Effects of Layoffs on Others." *California Management Review,* Winter 1992, pp. 9–27.

Brockner, J., and others. "Layoffs, Self-Esteem and Survivor Guilt: Motivational, Effective, and Attitudinal Consequences." *Organizational Behavior and Human Decision Processes,* 1985, (36), 229–244.

Brockner, J., and others. "Layoffs, Equity Theory, and Work Performance: Further Evidence of the Impact of Survivor Guilt." *Academy of Management Journal,* 1986, *(29),* 373–384.

Byrd, R. "Corporate Leadership Skills, a New Synthesis." *Organizational Dynamics,* 1987, *16*(1), 34–43.

Cameron, K. S., Freeman, S. J., and Mishra, A. K. "Best Practices in White-Collar Downsizing: Managing Contradictions." *The Executive,* 1991, *(5)*3, 57–72.

Cameron, K. S., Kim, M. U., and Whetten, D. A. "Organizational Effects of Decline and Turbulence." *Administrative Science Quarterly,* 1987, *(32),* 222–240.

Covey, S. R. *The Seven Habits of Highly Effective People: Restoring the Character Ethic.* New York: Simon & Schuster, 1989.

Davy, J. A., and Tansik, D. "Procedural Justice and Layoff Survival: Preliminary Evidence for the Effects of Voice and Choice and Survivors' Attitudes and Behavior." Unpublished manuscript, Arizona State University, Tempe, 1986.

Dorfman, J. R., "Heard on the Street." *Wall Street Journal,* Dec. 10, 1991, pp. C1–C2.

Drath, W. H., and Palus, C. J. *Leadership as Meaning Making in a Community of Practice.* Greensboro, N.C.: The Center for Creative Leadership, 1993.

Fenelon, F. *Playing for Time.* Saddle Brook, N.J.: American Book–Stratford Press, 1977.

Fink, S. L., Beak, J., and Taddeo, K. "Organizational Crisis and Change." *The Journal of Applied Behavioral Science,* 1971, *(7)*1, 15–37.

Flint, J. "Who Gets the Parachutes?" *Forbes,* Jan. 12, 1987, pp. 38–40.

Fowler, E. M. "Survivors' Syndrome in Layoffs." *New York Times,* June 3, 1986, p. D23.

Gottesfeld, H. *Abnormal Psychology: A Community Mental Health Perspective.* Chicago: Science Research Associates, 1979.

Hallett, J. J. "Worklife Visions." *Personnel Administrator*, 1987, (32)5, 56–65.

Harvey, J. B. *Management and Marasmus.* Unpublished manuscript, George Washington University, Washington, D.C., 1981.

Harvey, J. B. "Eichmann in the Organization: Or You Have to Know Who You Are in Bed With; Otherwise You Can't Tell Whether You Are Making Love or Being Raped." Unpublished manuscript. George Washington University, Washington, D.C., 1985a.

Harvey, J. B. "Getting Eichmann out of the Organization: Or Some Thoughts on Developing an Organization of Love-Makers." Unpublished manuscript, George Washington University, Washington, D.C., 1985b.

Harvey, J. B. *The Abilene Paradox and Other Meditations on Management.* Lexington, Mass.: Lexington Books, 1988.

Herzberg, F. "The Motivation-Hygiene Concept and Problems of Manpower". *Personnel Administration*, 1964, (27)1, 3–7.

Hirsch, P. *Pack Your Own Parachute: How to Survive Mergers, Takeovers, and Other Corporate Disasters.* Reading, Mass.: Addison-Wesley, 1987.

Hirschowitz, R. G. "Addendum." A Special Feature of *The Levinson Letter.* Levinson Institute, Belmont, Mass.: 1974.

Hofstede, G. "Motivation, Leadership, and Organization: Do American Theories Apply Abroad?" *Organizational Dynamics*, 1980, 9(1), 42–63.

Kalish, R. A. *Death, Grief, and Caring Relationships.* (2d ed.) Monterey, Calif.: Brooks-Cole, 1985.

Kübler-Ross, E. *On Death and Dying.* New York: Macmillan, 1969.

Kübler-Ross, E., and Warshaw, M. *Working It Through.* New York: Macmillan, 1987.

Kuhn, T. S. *The Structure of Scientific Revolutions.* (2d ed.) Chicago: University of Chicago Press, 1970.

Leider, R. *Taking Charge.* Minneapolis, Minn.: The Inventure Group, 1992.

Lifton, R. J. *Death in Life: Survivors of Hiroshima*. New York: Random House, 1967.

Marks, M. L. "Regrouping After Downsizing: The O.D. Role." Presentation handout, O.D. Network Conference, Long Beach, Calif., 1991a.

Marks, M. L. "Viewpoints." *Los Angeles Times*, Jan. 6, 1991b. p. D7.

Marks, M. L., and Mirvis, P. "Rebuilding After the Merger: Dealing with Survivor Sickness." *Organizational Dynamics*, 1992, (21)2, 18–32.

Marrow, A. *The Practical Theorists: The Life and Work of Kurt Lewin*. New York: Basic Books, 1969.

Marshak, R. J., and Katz, J. H. "The Symbolic Side of OD." *OD Practitioner*, 1992, (24)2, 1–5.

Merry, U., and Brown, G. *The Neurotic Behavior of Organizations*. Cleveland, Ohio: Gestalt Institute Press, 1987.

Moses, J. L. "A Psychologist Assesses Today's AT&T Managers." *Teleconnect*, Mar. 1987, pp. 32–36.

Porter, L. "Some Extrapolations, Metaphors, and Inferential Leaps." *OD Practitioner*, 1978, (10),3, 3.

Prokesch, S. "Remaking the American CEO." *New York Times*, Jan. 25, 1987, p. F1.

Right Associates. *Lessons Learned: Dispelling the Myths of Downsizing*. (2d ed.) Philadelphia, Penn.: 1992.

Sahakian, W. S. *The History of Philosophy*. New York: HarperCollins, 1971.

Schaef, A. W. *Co-Dependence: Misunderstood – Mistreated*. San Francisco: HarperCollins, 1986.

Schulz, R., and Aderman, D. "Clinical Research and the Stages of Dying." *Omega*, May 1974, pp. 137–143.

Schwadel, F., Moffett, M., Harris, R., and Lowenstein, R. "Thousands Who Work on Shuttle Now Feel Guilt, Anxiety, and Fear." *Wall Street Journal*, Feb. 6, 1986, p. 27.

Solzhenitsyn, A. I. *One Day in the Life of Ivan Denisovich*. Westport, Conn.: Praeger, 1963.

Solzhenitsyn, A. I. *The Gulag Archipelago 1918–1956: An Experiment in Literary Investigation.* New York: HarperCollins, 1974.

Tichy, N. M., and Devanna, M. A. *The Transformational Leader.* New York: Wiley, 1986.

Tillich, P. *The Courage to Be.* New Haven, Conn.: Yale University Press, 1952.

Tornow, W. W., and De Meuse, K. P. "The Tie That Binds Has Become Very, Very Frayed." *Human Resources Planning Society,* 1990, (13)3, 203–212.

Vaill, P. B. "Process Wisdom for a New Age." In J. D. Adams (ed.), *Transforming Work: A Collection of Organizational Transformation Readings.* Alexandria, Va.: Miles River Press, 1984.

Wellins, R. S., Byham, W. C., and Wilson, J. M. *Empowered Teams: Creating Self-Directed Work Groups That Improve Quality, Productivity, and Participation.* San Francisco: Jossey-Bass, 1991.

Whyte, W. H. *The Organization Man.* New York: Simon & Schuster, 1956.

Wilson, S. *The Man in the Gray Flannel Suit.* New York: Simon & Schuster, 1955.

Wyatt Company. "Restructuring—Cure or Cosmetic Surgery: Results of Corporate Change in the '80s with RXs for the '90s." Published survey report. Washington, D.C.: The Wyatt Company, 1991.

Index